Sandy Hook
A Man Sold A Gun

Michael R. Weisser

in collaboration with

William A. Weisser

Volume 7: Guns in America

Published by:

TeeTee Press
Ware MA 01082

ISBN: 0692945024
ISBN-13: 978-0692945025

Library of Congress Control Number: 2017913678

10 9 8 7 6 5 4 3 2 1

First Edition

DEDICATION

Sherrill Clement Smith
revered memory.

Dennis Healey & Kenneth Wilkinson
forever friendships.

Acknowledgements

Carolyn Goldstein
Phyllis Katz
Leonard Mermelstein
Deborah Smotiler

CONTENTS

INTRODUCTION   1

1   A MAN WITH A GUN   11

2   A MAN WITH MANY GUNS   38

3   A GUN   71

4   THE BLAME GAME BEGINS   98

5   THE BLAME GAME GETS WORSE   129

6   WHAT HAPPENED AT SANDY HOOK   159

POSTSCRIPT   180

NOTES AND REFERENCES   190

Introduction

At 9:30 a.m. on Friday, December 14, 2012, the Principal of Sandy Hook Elementary School in Newtown, CT, Dawn Hochsprung, sat down at a conference table for a Planning and Placement Team meeting. The purpose of the meeting, which was also attended by the school psychologist, a parent and several other staff members, was to discuss how to deal with students whose physical, mental or psychological problems created needs for special attention during the school day. For the Principal, these meetings were considered very important, a reflection of her personal commitment to the well-being of every child who attended her school.

Ninety miles away, in a strip mall off of Interstate 91 in East Windsor, CT, Dave Laguercia had just finished eating breakfast in the Sky Diner Restaurant, then walked next door to open his retail store. The store was named Riverview Sales, and it was the largest gun shop in Northern Connecticut with an inventory that attracted buyers from every part of the state. One of those buyers who lived in Newtown, less than five miles from the Sandy Hook Elementary School, was a woman named Nancy Lanza, who came up to the shop in March 2010, and bought a Sig 226 pistol, then returned in 2011 and bought a Bushmaster assault rifle known as the XM-15.

Back to December 14, 2012. Just as Dawn Hochsprung was starting her meeting, a number of explosions and the crashing of glass were heard from down the hall. Along with others, the Principal ran into the hallway to find herself looking at a young man a wearing a hat and sunglasses who pointed a rifle at her and began pulling the trigger. The 47-year old educator died instantly. Within ten minutes, twenty first-grade schoolchildren and six adults, including the Principal were killed, then the shooter pulled out a Glock 10 handgun and shot himself in the head.

The other pistol found on the body of the shooter was a Sig Model 226. By the afternoon of the shooting, the ATF had traced the Sig pistol first from the manufacturer to the wholesaler and then to the dealer who happened to be Dave Laguercia, owner of Riverview Sales. When an ATF agent called the store to verify the pistol sale, Dave informed the agent that he had also sold a Bushmaster assault rifle to the same buyer, a woman named Nancy Lanza who lived in

Newtown. And Dave made a point of telling the agent that Nancy Lanza had purchased both guns, because by the time he spoke to the ATF agent he already knew that the Sandy Hook shooter was her son, although the boy was still being misidentified as her older child Ryan, and that both mother and son were also dead.

The Sandy Hook massacre unleashed a firestorm of public anguish, anger and despair. The afternoon of the shooting, President Barack Obama spoke about the event on national television, saying, "our hearts are broken today -- for the parents and grandparents, sisters and brothers of these little children, and for the families of the adults who were lost." One week later, Wayne LaPierre of the National Rifle Association delivered a different message: "when it comes to the most beloved, innocent and vulnerable members of the American family – our children – we as a society leave them utterly defenseless, and the monsters and predators of this world know it and exploit it." These two statements would set the parameters of a public debate which then raged on for months.

The shooting at Sandy Hook wasn't the first mass shooting to send shockwaves through the public, nor was it the first mass shooting to take place inside a school. On April 20, 1999, two high school seniors, Eric Harris and Dylan Klebold, went into their high school in Columbine, CO, killed 12 students and one teacher, wounded 21 other people and then ended their lives by committing a double suicide. Eight years later, a senior at Virginia Tech University in Blacksburg shot 32 people to death and wounded 17 others before taking his own life.

What set Sandy Hook apart from those other shooting rampages, however, was the fact that most of the victims in the elementary school at Newtown were first graders whose young ages created an emotional tsunami that would not dissipate over time. Making the event more prominent was the fact that the location of the shooting was less than two hours' car ride from New York City. Which meant that within several hours the media descended on Newtown like a veritable invading force whose presence enlarged and then sustained the impact of the tragedy even further.

Meanwhile, at Riverview Sales and gun shops around the country, Friday started off with business as usual and as the day wore on, sales were stronger because the word was quickly beginning to get around within the gun industry that an event like Sandy Hook would create a public mood that might support increased regulation of guns. Following Barack Obama's brief but emotional address on December

14, the President came up to Newtown on Sunday to meet parents and family members of the victims, at which time he delivered a longer speech and promised some kind of response: "In the coming weeks, I'll use whatever power this office holds to engage my fellow citizens, from law enforcement, to mental-health professionals, to parents and educators, in an effort aimed at preventing more tragedies like this, because what choice do we have?"

What those remarks meant to gun dealers like Laguercia was the possibility of more government regulations over sales and ownership of guns, and more regulations would ultimately mean fewer guns. That Newtown was located in a strongly-Democratic and pro-regulation state was also not lost on gun dealers like Laguercia, who knew that a liberal, Democratic Governor like Dannel Malloy wouldn't let this event go by without making some kind of effort to tighten gun ownership in Connecticut through legislative means.

Because the gun industry is highly-regulated at the point of sale (you cannot purchase a new consumer product called a 'gun' unless you are first legally vetted and approved to do so) the financial health and welfare of people within the industry can be strongly impacted by political reactions to unpredictable events totally beyond their control.

Whenever a high-profile shooting hits the national news, gun sales spike upwards because gun owners immediately assume that the political reaction to the event will end up making it more difficult for them to own guns. On November 21, 1963, for example, who could have predicted that Americans would no longer be able to buy rifles and shotguns from the Sears catalog because a resident of Dallas purchased a World War II surplus Italian army carbine from a mail-order sporting goods dealer in Chicago and then used the gun on November 22 to kill the 35th President of the United States?

The narrative which first emerged from Sandy Hook was a narrative about victims, both the victims who were shot with an AR-15, and the victim who used the gun. The fact that a 20-year old first shot his mother dead in her bed before loading his shooting gear into his car and driving to the school not only added Nancy Lanza to the long list of victims, but was also cited as proof that Adam Lanza was a victim of his own mental distress. Less than 48 hours after the gunfire came to an end, Connecticut's Governor Dannel Malloy was talking on television about the trauma suffered by family and friends of the staff, teachers and students at Sandy Hook, as well as the unfortunate failure of the state's mental health system to treat Adam Lanza's mental problems, which otherwise might have kept the tragedy from taking place. Within a week after the shooting rampage, the popular magazine Psychology Today was promoting the idea that Lanza might have been an undiagnosed schizophrenic which made him a serious risk if he had access to guns.

Two years later, on November 21, 2014, the State of Connecticut's Office of the Child Advocate released its official assessment of the mental status and history of the shooter, Adam Lanza, which found that he had been "completely untreated in the years before the shooting" for both physical and psychiatric ailments and also failed to receive recommended mental services and drugs. A year earlier, the discussion of Adam Lanza's mental state in the official report about Sandy Hook issued by Connecticut's Division of Criminal Justice basically said the same thing.

Going back to the time of the event itself however, something as horrific as the Newtown slaughter was not going to be understood, accepted or rationalized away unless a 'bad guy' was identified who could be publicly blamed and punished for what had occurred. Within one week after Adam Lanza used the Bushmaster rifle which his mother purchased at Riverview to mow down teachers, staff and kids, Dave Laguercia would find himself the object of a legal assault by the full force and authority of the United States government once officials decided that the narrative coming out of Sandy Hook had to identify and vilify someone whose behavior could be seen as having caused or contributed to the horrendous event.

This book is an account of what happened to David Laguercia once it was decided that someone had to pay a price both for the deaths at Sandy Hook as well as the public trauma which then quickly spread throughout the United States. The reaction was so intense and widespread that it not only for the first time created a national, grass-roots movement for more restrictive gun laws, but also gave birth to a bizarre, media enterprise founded on the idea that the entire episode at Newtown was nothing but a hoax.

This book will cover those developments, including the various conspiracy theories which circulated and still circulate around Sandy Hook. I will show both why and how these conspiracy narratives appeared as well as well the degree to which they were all without any foundation at all. But the book will also describe the one, real conspiracy which developed after Sandy Hook, a conspiracy created, fostered and managed by federal law enforcement officials in order to convince a shocked and aggrieved public that something would be done.

This conspiracy, which has never previously been mentioned, had at its center the dealer who legally sold the gun that was used to murder 26 adults and kids, a totally-contrived story which continued for 16 months from the first media reports after the shooting, including the computer feed that Dave Laguercia was watching inside his store. For selling a legal product to a consumer and selling it following exactly the rules and regulations which governed such sales, Dave lost his entire business and millions of dollars in sales, inventory and future profits, lost his reputation, spent thousands of dollars on legal fees and now sits at home still waiting for the legal aftermath of Sandy Hook to come to an end.

In addition to following Dave's story, the book will also look at the controversies spawned by Sandy Hook, including mental illness and gun violence, lethality of assault-style weapons, effectiveness of gun regulations, protection by armed citizens and elimination or expansion of gun-free zones. These issues came to define and still define the national gun debate which erupted after Sandy Hook, and every one of these issues played a role in shaping Dave Laguercia's experiences from the moment he realized that the gun used in the shooting had come from his store. But what happened to Dave over the next several years was not just what can happen to someone caught in the vortex of unexpected events, it also reflects the degree to which we as a society and a culture demand explanations even for events we cannot predict, prevent or even understand.

The first thing we do not understand is why Adam Lanza took the rifle his mother purchased from Dave LaGuercia and drove from their house to Sandy Hook Elementary School. That's how the story begins.

CHAPTER 1

A MAN WITH A GUN

09:36:06 Newtown Police Dispatch broadcasts that there is a shooting at SHES. (Newtown radio)

9:36:06 Dispatcher Nute: "67 (Officer McGowan) Sandy Hook School caller is indicating she thinks there is someone shooting in building."

9:36:38 Newtown Sgt Kullgren hears broadcast and is enroute to SHES: (Newtown radio) Newtown Sgt Kullgren: "S6, I am enroute."[1]

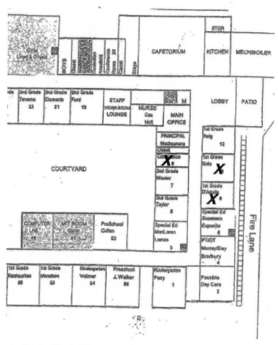

Figure 1. Sandy Hook Elementary School. Lanza enters through Lobby, shoots two adults coming out of Conference Room #9, then shoots teachers and students in Classrooms #8 and #10. From: State of Connnecticut, Division of Criminal Justice, Appendix to Sandy Hook Report, P. A116.

The young man who shot his way into Sandy Hook Elementary School on the morning of December 14, 2012, was born in New Hampshire but raised in Newtown, CT and attended Sandy Hook Elementary School. He was the son of Peter and Nancy Lanza whose marriage split up in 2001 when Adam was nine years old. We obviously have no descriptions of

Adam's childhood from his mother, but his father, who was interviewed at length a year after the shootings, said his son was an 'average child,' perhaps somewhat 'weird,' but nothing which could have been seen as turning him into the mass killer which he then became.

Peter Lanza's interview became the basis of a lengthy story which appeared in an issue of *The New Yorker Magazine* in March, 2014.[2] After his parents separated, Adam along with his older brother Ryan, continued to see their father on a regular basis, but this relationship was broken when Ryan left to go away to college and Peter and Nancy finalized their divorce in 2009. Beginning at that point Adam increasingly refused to see his father, a situation that may have been exacerbated by Peter's remarriage in 2010. Adam's distance from his father was part of a generalized withdrawal from family and social contacts, although he was still going to a video-game center and other locations up to the day he shot his way into the Sandy Hook school.

What is most telling about the Peter Lanza interview was the fact that, given his lack of contact with Adam after 2010 along with the death of his ex-wife, it would be virtually impossible for anyone to create a detailed or even vague personal profile of Adam's behavior and mind-set in the weeks and days leading up to the massacre at Sandy Hook. But this absence of parental and social engagement should not be taken to mean that Adam Lanza's mental condition hadn't been the subject of endless and continuous interventions both with public institutions, private therapists and other mental health professionals prior to the rampage on December 14, 2012.

When Adam was three years old, he was evaluated and consequently began receiving special education services which consisted of speech support and occupational therapy because he began talking late.[3] He was evaluated again in 1997 on an independent basis as requested by his parents, a procedure which resulted in speech and language services because he continued to have problems communicating with others even though he had no trouble understanding what was being said to him.

Adam entered Sandy Hook Elementary School in 1998. He was reading at grade level and was above grade level in math. His initial education plan called for continued therapy to develop fine motor skills and speech articulation and he was removed from special ed service in 4th grade after he met the requirements in reading and math of the Level 4 Connecticut Mastery Test. With one exception, there was nothing in Adam's behavior or school record which indicated mental problems between the ages of five and ten. The one exception was a picture book he authored with another student in the fifth grade which contained violent images and narratives about child murder and cannibalism which may have been more the work of the co-author but was not considered to be a serious indication of possible adverse or dangerous behavior at the time.

In 2004 when Adam was in 7th grade, his mother abruptly withdrew him from the public middle school and enrolled him in a local Catholic school. His report card at the end of 7th grade showed solid academic work but he left that school at the end of the Spring term and began home schooling in the 8th grade. In September 2005, Nancy Lanza appeared at the Danbury Hospital Emergency Room with Adam for what was described as a 'crisis' visit but was, in effect, her attempt to get a mental diagnosis which would allow her to keep and teach Adam at home.

The diagnosis that Adam received was 'Asperger Syndrome and Obsessive-Compulsive Disorder' which was then accepted by the Sandy Hook school system as a basis for Adam to be home schooled. Although treatment records were never made available, Adam saw a community psychiatrist for as many as 20 visits between 2005 and 2008. In a letter to the Newtown School Board, the psychiatrist confirmed the Asperger's diagnosis, noted that Adam might become extremely anxious if any routine was changed, and supported Nancy Lanza's request that Adam be allowed to learn at home.

On October 24, 2006 Adam was evaluated by a clinic psychiatrist and out of this experience he began treatments with an Advance Practice Registered Nurse (APRN) who was the coordinator of the Pervasive Developmental Delay (PDD) group at the Yale clinic, sessions which occurred simultaneously with continued visits to the community psychiatrist. Both Adam's mother and father were also engaged in discussions with this professional. Ultimately it was decided that Adam would work with one therapist, the community psychiatrist, and the APRN concluded that perhaps Adam wasn't suffering from Asperger's syndrome (which had had been renamed Autism Spectrum Disorder) but from disabling anxiety and Obsessive-Compulsive Disorder. There were also repeated contacts between Adam's parents and the Newtown School System as well as inquiries to other community school systems.

Adam returned full-time to a regular school environment in 10th Grade, and was at first integrated into a regular schedule of academic classes, along with extra-curricular activities, then began taking classes at Western Connecticut State University, accumulating enough classroom credits outside of the normal high school curriculum to graduate in June 2009, a year earlier than originally scheduled. Although he may have experienced difficulty in terms of interpersonal relationships as his high school experience came to an end, classmates interviewed after the shooting rampage considered him to be quiet but nevertheless 'normal' both in and outside of class.

Clinical evidence about Adam Lanza's mental condition becomes sparse between the completion of high school in 2009 and the Sandy Hook tragedy largely due to the fact that he increasingly appears to have isolated himself at home, connected with peers only through the internet, ended contact with his father and, of course, was not survived by his mother. But the information that we do possess indicates that in the years before he ended his own life and the lives of 27 others, he was examined and treated multiple times by experienced, mental health professionals, continuously observed by educators and lived in a stable, home environment with parents who were concerned throughout his entire life about his mental and physical growth and development.

What I have just said about Adam Lanza's personal history prior to his killing spree could be said, with few differences, about many, if not most of the rampage shooters who committed acts of mass murder both before and after Sandy Hook. On April 16, 2007 a college student named Seung-Hui Cho walked into two separate buildings on the Virginia Tech University campus in Blacksburg, VA, shooting a Glock pistol at everyone he saw. By the time he finished his spree by shooting himself, he had killed 32 people and actually set a new record for the number of killings by one individual which is now held by the late Omar Mateen walked into an Orlando nightclub and shot 49 people to death in June, 2016.[4]

Seung-Hui's family emigrated from Seoul, Korea to Maryland in 1992 when Seung-Hui was eight years old. They moved to Fairfax County, VA, the following year where both parents found work in the dry-cleaning business and their son was enrolled in public school. While attending the sixth grade, Seung-Hui began receiving counseling at the Center for Multi-Cultural Human Services on the recommendation of school staff who were concerned about his general social withdrawal and suicidal/homicidal ideations found in writing assignments, including school essays about Columbine. The diagnosis from the Center was 'selective mutism,' he was prescribed an anti-depressant to which he responded positively and medications were then stopped.

During high school Seung-Hui continued to receive therapy because of his shyness but was not considered a behavior problem and graduated with a 3.5 Honors GPA in June 2003. He then enrolled at Virginia Tech, majoring in business information systems but switched his major to English at the beginning of his junior year. He had spent his sophomore year in an off-campus apartment but then moved back into a campus dormitory beginning with the Fall Semester of 2005. Other than being still shy and aloof in personal relations, there was no indication of mental problems until Seung-Hui started his junior year.

Problems first surfaced in a course taught by the noted poet, Nikki Giovanni, who believed that Seung-Hui's behavior was considered a threat by other students and following a confrontation in the classroom, got Seung-Hui removed from the class.[5] Beginning in late November and through mid-December, University authorities were made aware of 'annoying' emails and texts received by various female students which were evidently sent under various aliases by Seung-Hui Cho. The campus police warned him to desist from such behavior on December 13, one of his suitemates in the dorm then received an IM in which Seung-Hui threatened suicide, the recipient notified campus cops and Cho ended up being detained overnight (under a magistrate's order) at the Carilion St. Alban's Psychiatric Center where he was evaluated and released the next day.

The evaluation conducted prior to Cho's release concluded that he was not a danger to himself or others, but recommended outpatient counseling which was incorporated into the magistrate's order releasing the patient who kept one appointment with the on-campus counseling center although no further mental health contacts were made. This is the last time that the record shows any behavioral issues between Cho and members of the University faculty, staff or student body, except for a brief argument with a professor about a writing assignment which the faculty member did not feel was serious enough to report.

Between February and April 2007, which was Seung-Hui's senior year, he legally purchased two pistols, loads of ammunition and sets of chains from Home Depot which he would later use to lock classroom doors from the inside while he was engaged in firing at persons within each room. The night before his rampage, Seung-Hui made his weekly, Sunday-night telephone call to his parents in Fairfax County, who later reported that the conversation was completely normal and did not raise any suspicions at all.

The next morning, at roughly 7 A.M., Cho entered the West Ambler Johnston dorm and shot two people, a female undergraduate and a male staff member. He then went back to his dorm (the bodies were discovered in Johnston Hall while Cho was back in his own dorm), meanwhile classes continued as usual while the police began a search for the boyfriend of the dead female student because another student told them that the boy was 'into guns.'

Two hours later, Cho appeared in Norris Hall, a building which contains classrooms used by the Engineering and other Departments, walked into Room 206 and began shooting the place up. He killed the professor and nine students, wounded three others, then walked across the hall to Room 205, again shot the faculty member (in a German language class) and attending students, exited Room 205, forced his way into another classroom where he continued shooting, but upon hearing police entering the building, turned the Glock on himself and shot himself in the head.

The entire episode took about 10 minutes and might have been an even briefer interval with less loss of life except that Seung-Hui had chained the entrance doors to Norris Hall shut from the inside which forced the police to first try and find an alternate entrance which they needed to blast their way through with a shotgun because they didn't have a key. It is presumed that Cho took his own life when he heard the report of the shotgun and knew that the police were on the scene. In all, Seung-Hui Cho killed 30 people besides himself.

On July 20, 2012, a 24-year old graduate student in neuroscience at the University of Colorado's Anschutz Medical Campus at Aurora, CO, went into a Century 16 movie theater showing the Batman superhero movie, *The Dark Knight Rises*, and proceeded to shoot 70 people with a Glock pistol, a Remington shotgun and a Smith & Wesson AR-15 assault rifle, of whom 12 died from their wounds.[6] The shooter, James Holmes, had previously checked out the theater and made it the target of his attack because he was able to enter and exit the building unobserved through a back door. He could also park his car near the door which made it easier for him to walk from his car to the building while carrying multiple guns, ammunition and other paraphernalia, including smoke grenades that he set off inside the theater to make it more difficult for anyone to witness what was going on.

Holmes was arrested standing next to his car and thus is one of the few rampage shooters whose behavior and mental history before the attack can be analyzed and understood. But from the night of the shootings until his trial and sentencing was completed on August 7, 2015, evidence and testimony about his degree of mental impairment was sometimes elusive, sometimes contradictory, and sometimes could not be connected in any way to what happened in the Century 16 theater the night of July 20, 2012.

Four months before his trial, the court having rejected an attempt by Holmes to plead not guilty by reason of insanity, *Psychology Today* carried an article about him in which the writer, a psychiatrist named Dale Archer, actually had the honesty and presence of mind to admit that he really couldn't make any definitive statements about the shooter's mental condition because he had 'neither seen nor evaluated Mr. Holmes. This is something a family therapist and psychologist named Jamie Turndorf, didn't bother to mention when she wrote an article about Adam Lanza's mental condition which also appeared in *Psychology Today*.[7]

This issue of making statements and judgements about the mental state of various individuals has long been a problem for the mental health community, particularly when the individual who is the subject of such discussions is either a high-profile shooter or even President of the United States. Most mental health professionals still abide by what is known as the 'Goldwater rule,' which is the American

Psychiatric Association's guideline stating that it is unethical (but not forbidden) to give a professional opinion about someone whom they have not personally examined.[8] In the case of Holmes, however, we have one of the few instances in which a mass shooter survived the event, but even in the aftermath of the rampage and leading up to the trial, the information which circulated about his mental status prior to the night of July 20, 2012, could hardly be considered a definitive statement about whether he should have been considered mentally impaired or not.

What we do know about the Aurora shooter is that Holmes was being treated by a University psychiatrist at the time of the actual mass murder event. A month prior to the rampage, this psychiatrist, Lynne Fenton, M.D., sent a message to the University police indicating that Holmes had made homicidal statements in a therapy session, but in her testimony during the trial, Dr. Fenton dismissed the idea that Holmes was an 'immediate' risk because his homicidal comments were a 'generalized' response to questions about his own personality and didn't indicate any kind of actual, homicidal plan.[9] Did she question Holmes about whether or not he was considering such behavior even though at the same time, unbeknownst to her, he had already amassed the arsenal he would use to perpetrate his theater attack? No such question was asked during her testimony and there's no reason to believe that he would have necessarily answered honestly even if he had been directly asked. During the trial, the University of Colorado released nearly 3,800 emails that were sent or received by Holmes through his university email accounts. Every email that mentioned anything about his mental status was redacted from public view.

On May 23, 2014, a 22-year old college dropout, Elliot Rodger, stabbed and killed his two roommates plus a friend in his apartment in the Santa Barbara suburb of Isla Vista, CA, then drove through the town, shooting three other people, wounding 7 others with gunfire and another 7 by striking them with his car, then took his own life after exchanging gunfire with local cops.[10] This rampage, from the time that Rodger stopped off at a Starbucks at 9:00 P.M. to get coffee, until he shot himself with his Sig P226 pistol, lasted slightly more than 30 minutes, but we do not know how much time elapsed between the killings of the three young men in Rodger's apartment until he began driving around town.

Once again the general public was treated to a detailed analysis of this mass shooter's alleged mental illness in the pages of *Psychology Today* by a Professor of Philosophy at the University of Florida, Berit Brogaard, who holds a Danish graduate degree called a D.M.Sci, which I have never heard of previously, but evidently means something like Doctor of Medical Science, along with also having earned a regular Ph.D.[11] Having conducted an extensive investigation of Rodger's Facebook page and other media resources created and distributed by the shooter, but having never actually seen or evaluated Rodger himself, the esteemed Dr. Brogaard nevertheless concluded that he was suffering from 'narcissistic personality disorder' which of course made him a danger both to others and to himself.

In fact, Elliott Rodger was never diagnosed with 'narcissistic personality disorder.' In fact, in 2007 he was diagnosed with 'pervasive development disorder' which is today considered a not-unusual condition found on the autism spectrum, which also resulted in Rodger being prescribed anti-anxiety drugs, including Xanax, which he was still taking at the time of the shooting attacks. He was also continuously in therapy, largely due to his difficulty in making and maintaining friendships, in particular members of the opposite sex. He received a monthly allowance of $500 from his parents, some of which he used to purchase three different handguns, but at no time was he ever placed in a hospital setting of any kind due to mental illness or stress.

On April 30, 2014, three weeks before the rampage began, the crisis line of the Santa Barbara County Mental Health Department received a telephone call from Rodger's mother, who asked that the police be sent to her son's apartment to conduct a 'welfare check' because she was concerned about YouTube videos he had posted in which he appeared to be depressed. Six Sheriff's Department deputies then visited Rodger at his apartment and their report stated that the subject was "shy, timid and polite." He told them that the videos were just a way of expressing that he was having trouble being socially accepted in Isla Vista and in particular, meeting and dating girls. When the cops finished the interview, they called his mother who denied seeing anything in the videos which indicated that her son harbored homicidal/suicidal thoughts or plans.

Let's conclude this discussion of the mental status of people who commit mass killings by describing the gugga-mugga shooting rampage of them all, the killing of 15 people and wounding of another 21 victims by Eric Harris and Dylan Klebold at Columbine High School on April 20, 1999.[12] I don't know if Michael Moore's movie, *Bowling for Columbine*, is what has kept this mass shooting so uppermost in people's minds, or perhaps Moore took advantage of the degree to which the Columbine massacre marks a fundamental point of departure for the continued interest in this event (the mother of one of the shooters, Sue Klebold, gained enormous news coverage when she published a book about the incident in 2016.) Either way, any discussion about the how's and why's of mass shootings in America would not be complete without a discussion of this event.

On April 20, 1999, two Columbine High School students, Dylan Klebold and Eric Harris, both of whom about to graduate within the next three weeks, placed two home-made, propane bombs on the floor of the school cafeteria which were set to go off at 11 A.M. Their plan, which may have been in the works for as long as a year, was to wait outside the school and shoot at students whom they believed would run from the building when the bombs went off.

Except the bombs didn't go off. They turned out to be duds. So instead of waiting for students to come towards them, shortly after 11 A.M. Harris and Klebold walked towards the school shooting at every student in sight. Outside the building they shot seven students, of whom two died. Then they entered the cafeteria and quickly shot four more students and teachers, all of whom luckily would survive. So far the assault had lasted less than ten minutes and the toll was nine people wounded and two dead.

The gunmen had come into the school with two sawed-off shotguns and two assault weapons – a Tec 9 assault handgun and a Hi Point assault carbine, both with hi-cap, 9mm mags. They also carried pipe bombs which they set off in hallways while walking through the building from room to room. Entering the school library, they spent the next 7 minutes taunting students, making jokes about what they were doing, letting some leave the room but wounding 11 and killing 9 more.

By this time the school building had been evacuated except for shooting victims who were too injured to move under their own steam or with the help of others. Klebold and Harris wandered through the building for another ten minutes or so, igniting more explosives and then ending up back in the cafeteria where they took their own lives. The time elapsed between the first shot aimed at a student until the last round aimed at someone other than themselves was roughly 20 minutes. In all, they murdered 13 students and teachers and injured 21 others during the assault.

Like Sandy Hook and Virginia Tech, the suicide of the Columbine assailants precluded the possibility that any sort of definitive judgement could be made regarding the motives or psychological states of minds of either Klebold or Harris. Much of the post-incident commentary about them, however, was prompted by online stories, videos and digital publications which they produced in the run-up to the actual event.

There seems to be something of a repetitive pattern seen in these rampages which involves the production and sharing of detailed journals, essays and other forms of narratives that appear in the period prior to the shooting rampage itself. Klebold and Harris posted a website in 1996, which by early 1997 began to contain references to bomb-making, as well as random comments about the shortcomings of American society which needed to be arrested or changed through violent means. Elliot Rodger also posted an online diary that circulated on the internet after his rampage, and like the content of the Harris-Klebold website, contained allusions to violence and anger over the way Rodger was treated by some of his peers.

One year before their rampage, Klebold and Harris posted death threats on the website against another student, Brooks Brown. The website address was then given to Brown so that he could view the threats; he showed the site to his parents who then filed a complaint against Harris and Klebold with the

County Sheriff's Office. The investigator assigned to the case found threats against other students and teachers on the website but no further action occurred. In the aftermath of the shooting the lack of response to the Brown complaint would be cited as a missed intervention opportunity which might have prevented the school slaughter from going down.

At the beginning of February 1998, Harris and Klebold were arrested for stealing tools from an electrician's truck and sentenced to a 'diversion' program which required them both to attend behavior classes, including anger management class. Harris also briefly saw a psychologist who prescribed an anti-depressant that the patient may still have been taking in the months leading up to the attack. After their sentencing, the website containing insults and threats against other members of the Columbine school community, as well as content about bomb-making and other violence was taken down; obviously the boys were trying to divert public attention away from their plans.

The official report on Columbine released by the Governor's Office in 2001, noted that, "Although Dylan Klebold and Eric Harris outwardly appeared to be typical teenagers – both held part-time jobs and were on schedule to graduate with high school diplomas – there were indications that the pair had suicidal and violent tendencies. They expressed clear hatred for society in general and, beyond that, for all humankind."[13]

If I had a nickel for every kid who goes on the internet and posts videos or commentaries about violence or murder I could have retired years ago. As for suicide, there is no question that suicidal ideation, spoken or otherwise, could be a symptom of severe mental stress and should be attended to immediately whenever or wherever it crops up. But while guns are used in more than half of all successful suicides each year, and have become a more significant factor in teen and young adult suicides, rarely does someone who uses a gun to end their lives shoot other people before they commit their life-ending event.

When suicide is the culmination of an episode in which a gun causes the loss of multiple lives, invariably this kind of event occurs within the context of a family situation and doesn't involve the shooting of strangers or persons unknown to the shooter himself or themselves. The Columbine event, like the Virginia Tech massacre, obviously brought the shooters face-to-face with other students whom they might have known or at least recognized on a random basis. But with the exception of two Columbine students who recognized Klebold and Harris, exchanged brief words and were allowed to flee, there is no indication of the existence of personal relationships or familiarity between any of the shooters and any of the victims at either school.

Let's sum up what we know so far about the individuals who committed mass murder at Columbine, Virginia Tech, Aurora, Isla Vista, and Sandy Hook. The shooters were all males ranging between the ages of 17 and 24, they all had completed high school (or were about to complete it) and were either enrolled in college, had experienced college life or were planning to begin college years. They all came from stable, middle-class families and all of them (with the exception of Dylan Klebold) had been treated by mental health professionals for what in every single case was some degree of anti-social behavior that did not appear to represent any degree of serious threat.

Several months following the Columbine massacre, a national study group of experts convened not just to talk about what happened at the high school on April 20, 1999, but to develop a 'threat assessment perspective' which might alert schools and other institutions to the possibility of mass violence being committed in their midst.[14] The experts at this meeting included Dr. Frank Ochberg, whose world-class credentials in the fields of stress and trauma are without dispute, and FBI Special Agent Dwayne

Fuselier, who led the FBI investigation at Columbine and is a clinical psychologist to boot.

In interviews following the study group and in an official report, both Ochberg, Fuselier and other experts were clear on the degree to which rampage shooters were mentally ill. On the other hand, the type of illness from which the shooters suffered did not manifest itself in symptoms or behavior which could necessarily be identified to the point of predicting a violent attack. Regarding how to understand Columbine, it was argued that Eric Harris, the instigator and promoter, was a classic psychopath who used violence and murder to achieve certain ends without the slightest regard or concern for the victims who were killed. His behavior was certainly not 'normal' in any sense of the word, even though he may, in fact, have exhibited a clear understanding of what he was doing and what was going on.

The view of mental health experts is that rampage murderers are clearly mental cases, even if they behave normally up to the moment the rampage begins. Which is quite a different perspective from the consensus that has emerged over the years in the mental health community about the general question of gun violence and the mentally ill. As regards gun violence defined as mass, rampage shootings, mental health professionals do not regard these events as being within the usual construct used to understand the motives and behavior of shooters because they constitute such a small proportion of the total number of individuals who are injured or killed with guns. The problem which arises from mass shootings, according to mental health experts, is that such rampages catch public attention and lead the general public to assume that all injuries from guns follow from the same degree of mental illness which is obviously the case with the shooters who kill or injure twenty, thirty or fifty people at one time.

A recent summary of the link between mental illness and everyday gun violence states that "People with serious mental illness are rarely violent. Only 3%–5% of all violence, including but not limited to firearm violence, is attributable to serious mental illness."[15] This summary then goes on to list "Common Misperceptions" about gun violence, such as "Serious mental illness is one of the primary causes of gun violence in the United States." In other words, individuals who shoot 20 or 30 people at one time suffer from some kind of mental disease, but individuals who pull out a gun and attempt to kill another person more than 75,000 times each year are as sane and mentally normal as you and me.

The post-Columbine study group also found it imperative to respond to what they called 'misinformation about school shootings,' because "news coverage magnifies a number of widespread but wrong or unverified impressions of school shooters." And one of the mistaken impressions about the Columbine shooters and other school-based rampage killers was the belief, fostered by the media, that "easy access to weapons is THE most significant risk factor."

So, on the one hand, the public is told that people who commit 100,000 intentional gun homicides and non-fatal gun assaults every year are not, by and large, loony tunes, but the relatively few who use guns to commit mass murders are dangerous not because they can get their hands on a gun, but because they are suffering from mental illness which can only be diagnosed after the damage is done.

Let me present a contrary point of view which goes like this: Virtually all one-on-one shootings are impulsive acts whose 'trigger mechanisms' are no better understood or predictable than the behavior which drives individuals to shoot twenty or thirty people at one time. Unfortunately, this argument disappears because the public expects, indeed demands an explanation for rampage shootings while at the same time ignoring the banal, and unseen gun violence that occurs throughout the United States every day.[16]

The individual who ended up taking the blame in response to the public reaction after one of these 'crazy' killers who seemed normal before he shot his way down the hallway of a public school, was a gun dealer named Dave Laguercia who happened to have legally sold the shooter's mother a gun. But since according to the experts, easy access to guns is not a serious risk factor in explaining gun rampages, then why would anyone even care where the gun came from or how the gun was even used? This is what we will try to figure out in the remainder of this book as we begin to look at what happened to Dave Laguercia after he opened his gun shop on Friday, December 14, 2012.

Chapter 2

A Man With Many Guns

Dave Laguercia grew up knowing next to nothing about guns. He didn't even own a gun until he walked into a bric-a-brac store on a weekend when he had nothing to do, saw a couple of antique rifles leaning against a wall, made an offer and now he owned a couple of guns. He had no idea what kind of guns they were, had no idea what to do to get them to work, he just wanted to buy some junk and now he owned a couple of old, junk guns.

Dave's father was in the used car business and took Dave into the business when the kid finished school. The family lived in West Springfield, there were two sisters, parents and Dave in the household, he was raised just like any other kid. At some point he then went out on his own, opened a used car business, then expanded to a second lot, made a good living, got married, things went well.

In the 1990s, when Dave had been buying, selling and trading used cars for some twenty years, he began buying and selling used guns. First he sold some antiques, then some modern guns, added some accessories and ammunition and by around 2001 or 2002 got out of the car business and opened a cozy, retail gun store. He still lived near West Springfield but put his gun shop right over the state line in Connecticut where gun laws regulating dealers were somewhat less strict than in the state where he lived.

In particular, Connecticut unlike Massachusetts did not continue the Clinton assault weapon ban that had been passed in 1994 but expired a decade later unless a state, like Massachusetts, opted to continue the ban in effect. What this meant was that in Massachusetts, a new gun could only be sold with a magazine which held a maximum of 10 rounds, but magazines of any capacity could be legally sold in Connecticut, as well as popular, hi-capacity pistols like Springfield and Glock. Along with a wider choice of handgun inventory, gun dealers in Connecticut could also sell the increasingly popular military-style rifles known as the AR-15, and could equip those weapons with all kinds of accessories (folding stocks, bayonet lugs) and hi-capacity magazines which also could not be sold in states like Massachusetts which continued to enforce the 1994 assault weapons ban.

Having hung around used cars all his life, Dave was pretty good when it came to fixing and altering mechanical parts with his hands. And right around the time he opened his gun shop, gun makers were shifting towards polymer instead of steel frames, and such frames could be easily customized with accessories like lasers, lights and tactical (i.e., expensive) sights. The design of the increasingly-popular AR-15 rifle lent itself to customized work because you could not only add all kinds of doodads to the gun's frame, but also switch out barrels and whole frames as well. As long as the gun was sold with its original receiver (the part of the frame that contained the trigger mechanism) and original serial number, you could change the rest of the gun in as many different ways as you chose.

This kind of work was perfect for someone like Laguercia who had been playing around with mechanical parts almost since the day he was born. Very quickly his shop became known as a place to purchase customized assault rifles like the AR-15, business grew steadily and by 2005 Dave was ready to expand into a larger store.

Dave rented a good-sized retail space in a strip mall adjacent to an exit on I-91, which meant that gun nuts could easily get to his store from anywhere within the state. Connecticut is bisected by two interstate highways that cross each other at Hartford: I-84 which runs from the New York State line east of

Danbury to Boston, and I-91 that goes north-south from New Haven (where the highway connects to I-95) to the Massachusetts state line. From anywhere on either of these internet routes a driver is an hour or less from Dave's store. And gun nuts have a way of talking to other gun nuts, which is why Nancy Lanza, for example, would have driven close by at least 6 other gun retailers when she came up from Newtown to buy a pistol and again to buy a rifle in Dave Laguercia's store.

But before we get to those transactions, let's spend some more time talking about Dave. The store into which he moved and named Riverview Sales, contained an inventory of more than 1,000 guns and at least a half-million dollars of additional inventory – ammunition, holsters, targets, cleaning kits – covering some 4,000 square feet. In addition to Dave and his wife Randi, there were usually two or three other employees on duty at all times, a not-unusual situation given that this store was annually selling more than 5,000 guns.

From the day Dave opened Riverview and became one of the largest and busiest gun dealers in the Nutmeg State, he began to experience the bane of all large and successful gun shops, namely, the difficulty if not impossibility of controlling the immense amount of paperwork that is generated by the sale of guns. And since this paperwork became the basis upon which Dave was ultimately victimized because of the legal sale of an AR-15 to a woman from Newtown, it's important that we spend some time explaining what these paperwork issues in the gun business are all about.

If you go into a retailer, let's say Wal Mart, Target or the corner convenience store, the only paperwork that is created by the money you spend is the sales receipt which pops out of the register and states the name of the store, the date of the sale and the amount which has been 'tendered' (paid) as well as the proportion of that money which represents tax. If it's a large store or a chain operation, there may be additional data created for such things as tracking inventory, price histories and so forth, but at the end of the day when the retailer wants to know how well he did and where he stands, basically all he does is punch a button on his register which will give him a summary of the daily take. This documentation, incidentally, might be used for his tax returns and might, in rare instances become information that the state or the feds would examine if a store audit occurs.

As respects the information which must be created and retained in the gun business, however, those retailers operate in a world which is entirely alien and different from what goes on in every other type of enterprise whose revenues are derived from the transfer and payment for goods. First and most important, gun sellers are the only retailers who can only engage in selling after they have been given a federal dealer's license which requires a background check to make sure they are law-abiding enough to put their own hands on guns.

This procedure first started in 1938, when the Roosevelt Administration came up with the idea of federal gun-dealer licensing because it was a quick and easy way to raise some revenue for the cash-starved New Deal.[1] The annual license fee was a dollar, but what was much more onerous than the fee was the record-keeping requirement which imposed the responsibility of the dealer to note some identifiers (name, address) of everyone to whom a gun was sold. The law also created for the first time the notion of 'prohibited persons,' i.e., individuals whose legal history did not allow them to own guns, but dealers were not responsible for verifying whether their customers were, in fact, prohibited from being gun owners – complying with this part of the 1938 law was left up to the gun owners themselves.

The paperwork for the federal regulatory environment of gun commerce came into its own in 1968 with the passage of the Gun Control Act

(GCA68), whose main provisions remain the foundation for gun control at the national level to this day.[2] This law placed the Bureau of Alcohol, Tobacco and Firearms (ATF) squarely in charge of regulating and monitoring how guns moved from one place to another, as well as who could and could not purchase or own a gun. The documentation that was developed to cover these two activities – movement and ownership – was comprised of two parts. To regulate the movement of guns from one location to another, every holder of a federal firearms license had to maintain something called the Acquisition and Disposition list (A&D book) in which would be recorded the manufacturer or previous owner, model and serial number of every gun which entered or left any licensed location; to regulate who could and could not own a gun, a document known as the Form 4473 was put into play.

The A&D register contains two sides: the acquisition side where the dealer inscribes the date, gun maker, model, caliber and serial number of every gun received, as well as noting a name and complete address if the gun was given to him by an individual (for example, a used gun being taken in trade) or the name and federal firearms license number if the gun had been purchased from another license-holder, in most cases a gun wholesaler from whom the dealer purchased guns. When a gun then leaves the shop, either because it was purchased over the counter or was being sent to another dealer or shipped back to the factory for repair, the Disposition side of the ledger was then filled in with the name and address of the purchaser or the name and FFL number if the gun was sent to another federal licensee.[3]

When the ATF comes into a gun shop to conduct an inspection, the first thing they do is count the number of blank spaces on the Disposition side of the A&D book and then count the number of guns in the store. If the numbers are the same, then the A&D book contains an accurate record at that moment of the guns which have come into the shop at some point but have not yet left. On the other hand, if there are more blank spaces than guns on the premises, this suggests that some guns have left the shop without their disposition being recorded, which is a serious mistake because it may mean that these guns are either missing, lost or transferred without the identifying information which would disclose where the gun went. Either way, the dealer has not only failed to keep accurate records about the movement of his guns, but has committed a second mistake by not notifying the ATF in timely fashion about missing or stolen guns. The night the ATF raided Riverview the week following Sandy Hook, they informed the media during their inspection that they couldn't locate 50 guns. So they said.

If you think the A&D register creates paperwork issues for gun dealers, that's nothing compared to what dealers have to contend with when it comes to dealing with the ATF Form 4473.[4] And before you, the reader, start getting glassy-eyed at my detailed and overly-long discussion about paperwork, I need to remind you again that it was over a simple paperwork error that an entire conspiracy was put together to blame Sandy Hook on Dave Laguercia and the way he operated Riverview Sales. So understanding the details of the documentation which regulates the gun industry is essential to understanding how the regulators of that industry dealt with Dave.

The Form 4473 was developed by the ATF following the passage of the GCA68 law, because one of the major responsibilities which the law placed on gun dealers was the requirement that they play a primary role in attempting to keep guns out of the 'wrong hands.' And the categories of wrong hands which were initially defined in the 1938 gun-control law, felons and fugitives, was expanded in GCA68 to include habitual drug users, people who had been institutionalized for being mentally ill (the quaint term 'mental defective' is still on the current form) individuals dishonorably discharged from the armed forces and anyone renounced their citizenship and a few other bad things. Over the years since 1968 some additional categories have been added, including persons charged with domestic violence and stalking, as well as whether the individual is an alien or non-citizen illegally in the United States.

The problem with the 4473 form after 1968, however, was that the dealer was only responsible for making sure that the gun buyer answered all those questions, and then verified his or her identity with a government-issued ID. The purchaser also had to fill out basic personal information including address, date and place of birth, height, weight, race, ethnicity and gender, some of which the dealer could verify by comparing this information to the government-issued ID. So even if someone said they weighed 150 pounds, the dealer had to accept this answer as truthful even if the last time the guy standing in front of you weighed 150 pounds in his dreams.

In all, the purchaser has to fill out 30 different fields, then sign and date the form, which the dealer then has to also sign and date the form before a firearm could be released. This process became more complicated after the passage of the Brady bill in 1994, because in addition to checking the form to make sure it was filled out properly, the dealer could not release a gun until the FBI allowed the transfer to proceed following the dealer's contacting the FBI background check group in West Virginia, reading the personal information about the customer over the phone, and then filling in 10 more fields in the form and, if the transfer was delayed so that the FBI could perform a more extensive background check, ultimately filling in 5 or 6 more fields on the 4473.

By the time Dave Laguercia opened Riverview Sales in East Windsor, in order to receive and then sell a gun to anyone, he or one of his employees along with the customer had to enter more than 60 separate pieces of information on the A&D register and the 4473. Which meant that every year Dave, as the licensed dealer at Riverview, was responsible for the correctness of more than 300,000 pieces of information every year, insofar as each year he was selling roughly 5,000 guns.

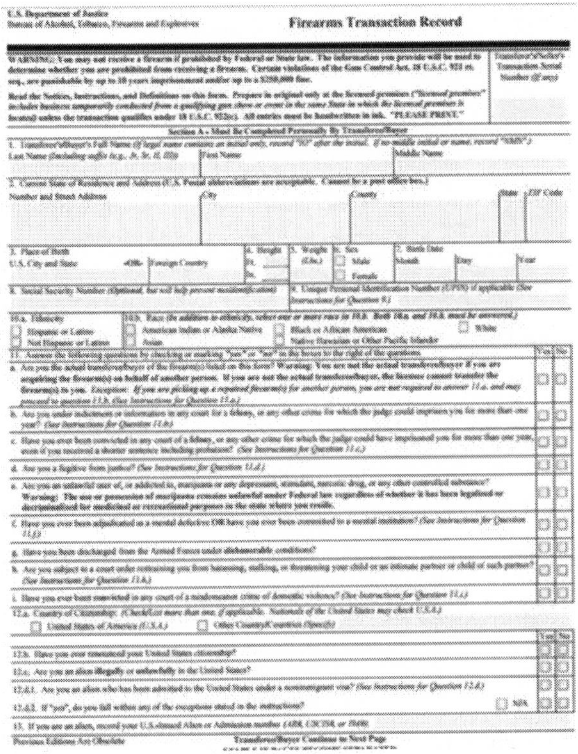
Firearms Transaction Record

Figure 2. ATF Form 4473 – front page.

A year prior to Sandy Hook, an ATF compliance team walked into Riverview one day and began an examination of his A&D register and his collection of 4473 forms. This procedure, known as an audit or an inspection, is the chief regulatory task of the ATF since GCA68 requires the agency to make sure that licensed dealers are complying with the law.[5] The ATF says they conducted 8,696 such inspection in 2015, which represents roughly 15% of the individuals who hold the federal firearms dealer's license (FFL) which is the license required to engage in retail gun sales.

Why is the ATF concerned about how federally-licensed dealers behave? Because the agency says that "It is critical that federal firearms licensees comply with the Gun Control Act of 1968, and its implementing regulations, in order to assist law enforcement efforts, prevent the diversion of firearms from lawful commerce to the illegal market, ensure successful tracing of firearms, and to protect the public." What we will see in the case of Riverview Sales was that the charges brought against Dave Laguercia had absolutely nothing to do with diversion of firearms or successful tracing of guns, but did allegedly involve a threat to public safety, which became the basis upon which the entire conspiracy against him was developed and hatched. But let's get back to the ATF inspection of Riverview's paperwork the year before Sandy Hook.

What was the possibility that the ATF inspection team wouldn't find some clerical errors in the forms that customers and staff filled out for the transfer each year of more than 5,000 guns? The possibility was zero. It simply would not be possible for a retail operation that was transferring 15 guns, on average, every day, along with accessories, ammunition and other retail items, to make sure that 60 error-free fields could be filled out *by hand* every time a gun went out the door.

Some information was obviously more important than other information. For example, Dave was obsessive about making sure that no gun left the store unless a release had been received from the FBI. He also installed and continuously ran a sophisticated video system because at one point he had been victimized in his first store by an employee who stole some guns (all of which were recovered when Dave viewed the daily video and saw the guy exiting the premises with several guns.) Given the size and complexity of the store inventory, not just guns but everything else, he also used a computer-based, point-of-sale system which contained information on all guns that was entered into the system when guns arrived and then updated when guns were sold to customers and taken away. Finally, and this is an important point that will come back when we talk about what happened in the store after Sandy Hook, Dave had also put his A&D book online, which meant he could search for information on any gun he had sold both by identifiers linked to the gun itself, as well as to the customer who purchased any particular gun.

When the ATF finished their inspection of Riverview, to nobody's surprise they discovered various clerical errors in the A&D and 4473 data, but they did not find any evidence that guns were either missing from the store or had been taken out of the store without first qualifying the buyer through the FBI background check. Because there were paperwork errors, Laguercia found himself in the never-never land which the ATF has created to decide whether a licensed dealer's behavior and compliance with regulations creates any degree of risk.

The Alice in Wonderland nature of ATF compliance regulations can be found in the agency's comments about FFL revocations, which cite "failure to account for firearms, failure to verify and document purchaser eligibility, failure to maintain records requisite for successful firearms tracing, and failure to report multiple sales of handguns" as the usual reasons for taking disciplinary action against a federally-licensed dealer.[6] In fact, Laguercia's inspection did not turn up any such violations and he was allowed to continue operating his business after attending several conferences at the ATF office in Hartford where the paperwork errors found in the inspection were reviewed and he agreed to be more diligent in recordkeeping going forward. Following the audit, he hired an industry-approved consulting firm to both monitor the store's recordkeeping, as well as to train all store employees in compliance rules and best practices.

On the other hand, and here comes the looking-glass, the federal code covering GCA68 says that any willful violation of any section of the law could be punished by five years in jail, however, the ATF admits that they have never defined a 'willful' violation, so they refer to case law, which they say defines willfulness as "the intentional disregard of a known legal duty or plain indifference to a licensee's legal obligations." Now that's clear, isn't it? Obviously, whatever mistakes were uncovered in the ATF's inspection of Riverview were not considered willful enough to merit any disciplinary action, and Laguercia was allowed to continue operating his business in the usual way.

In August 2010, a former employee of a Hartford beer distributorship, Omar Thornton, was called into the manager's office and told he could either resign or be fired because he had evidently been seen stealing beer from the warehouse.[7] After signing a resignation document which had been prepared in advance, Thornton went back to his locker, took a pistol out of his lunchbox, killed eight employees, wounded two others and then shot himself in the head. As we will see in Chapter 4, this mass shooting would be linked both to Sandy Hook and Laguercia, because in the coverage of the Newtown shooting, media outlets stated that like Nancy Lanza, Thornton had also bought his gun at Riverview, thus picturing Laguercia as a man who specialized in selling mass murder guns.

The only problem was that this story was simply not true. In fact, the gun Thornton used to shoot his way through the Budweiser distributorship had been purchased in a gun store located south of Hartford in Newington, indeed the owner of that store spoke with Dave after the ATF showed up at his shop and told him that personal papers found on Thornton included a sales receipt for ammunition from Dave's gun shop, which had nothing to do with the purchase of the gun.

The fact that an examination of Riverview's records would have shown that the shop was not the source of Thornton's gun made absolutely no difference when the ATF decided in 2012 to make Dave the 'bad guy' for the events at Sandy Hook. And it is exactly because of stories like the story about where Thornton bought his gun which, when gun dealers think about the ATF, their thoughts are a combination of fear and dread. Because the ATF has a virtual carte blanche to decide for itself what it can and can't do to the gun dealers whose business practices and behavior they regulate based on the authority granted the agency in GCA68. And even though a law was passed in 1986 which revised certain parts of GCA68 as it concerned regulatory activities, revisions based on credible reports that ATF agents were abusing their authority both against gun dealers and individual gun owners, the agency basically continues to operate in ways which leave too much unknown and too much unsaid.[8]

In 2014 the ATF conducted an inspection of a very active gun shop in Virginia, SSG Tactical, which sells more than 7,000 guns each year and is particularly known for its inventory of 'black' (assault-style) guns and Class III (full-auto) weapons. The shop had been in business for 20 years, there were no issues with law enforcement or anything like that, and when the ATF completed their audit after more than six months, they had identified 180 errors on various 4473 forms, an accuracy rate of 99.98 percent. The ATF did not find a single gun that had been released without a background check, nor were any guns missing from store inventory when the inspection commenced.

So SSG Tactical was allowed to stay in business following their audit, and the ATF lived up to its self-described objectives "to educate the licensee about regulatory responsibilities and to evaluate the level of compliance." Except what also happened and was not reported by the ATF or anyone else is that SSG estimates it cost close to $100,000 in additional salary to cover the time that employees went back to check the correctness of every, single piece of auditable paper because the store would be audited again the following year and if any violations were discovered, even violations which the ATF did not pick up in their previous audit, such violations would be considered 'willful' and the store could be shut down.[9]

There's one other hidden cost to ATF audits which is another reason why gun dealers think about the ATF in Hunter Thompson-esque 'fear and loathing,' terms, and the problem goes like this. The ATF investigators, known as Industry Operations Investigators (IOI) don't call up ahead of time to let the gun shop know when they are planning to show up. After all, if they did that, for all they know, the dealer would immediately conduct a complete review of his entire paperwork to make sure it was up to snuff. Yea, right. In fact, the IOI team walks in unannounced, they hang around for as long as they like, and because they don't bring bag lunches (after all, they are well-paid professionals) they come and go as they please.

The bottom line is that the inspection of a good-sized store probably involves twenty different days in which ATF agents are on the premises of the gun shop whose ongoing business activity they can observe and inspect, and when the average gun guy walks into a gun shop, the last thing he's going to do is buy a gun when the ATF is around. How do I know this? Because my gun shop was inspected by the ATF over a period of four months, indeed it was inspected by the same IOI group which audited Riverview Sales, and during that time my gun sales, which usually averaged about 25 a week, simply collapsed.

You might ask how come folks don't want to buy guns just because some ATF agents are on the scene? And the answer is very simple, namely, that most gun owners believe, with good reason, that the role of the ATF is to help the government get rid of guns. And this belief is the reason why organizations that work to reduce gun violence are wasting their time trying to figure out a way of talking about gun control that won't piss off 'responsible' gun owners, because there must be lots of people out there who understand the risk of owning guns.

Know what? A lot of people understand the risks of smoking and still smoke. Ditto people who exceed the speed limit. And most of all, people who just can't get rid of that extra weight still know they are at risk for heart disease, diabetes, stroke, and God knows what else. All I know is every time the ATF boys (and girls) showed up at my shop to continue their inspection of my books, customers came in and looked around but they didn't buy. And I'd be willing to bet you that this has been the experience of every gun shop owner who ever had to put up with the ATF. Sure, I was polite, I was friendly, I even gave the IOI squad a table and chairs where they could work. But I didn't want them in my shop and I didn't like them being in my shop.

On the other hand, as long as I had an active FFL, I couldn't tell them to leave because the way the law works, the documentation which I have to keep on the premises for them to examine can be examined by them at any time, for as long as they choose. In effect, I'm not the owner of these documents, I'm the custodian and the ATF determines how good my custodianship behavior has been.

One day in September, 2013 the IOI gang marched into my store without warning, showed me their little plastic IOI identify cards and proceeded to get to work. I had gone through a brief audit back when I took over the shop from the previous owner in 2001, just a month or so before the Twin Towers came down. Since that time my A&D book had collected somewhere around 11,000 – 12,000 entries, of which 200 guns were sitting in the shop. After my

A&D register was examined and the number of blank disposition spaces was compared to the number of guns in the store, it was determined that I was missing two guns, one of which it turned out was in a gun safe next to the retail counter, which brought those two missing guns down to one.

The ATF folks left and returned several days later to begin checking my 4473 forms, both to make sure that every 4473 was filled out correctly, that no guns had been released without a completed background check, and the information about the buyer matched the information for that particular sale entered in the A&D. This process took somewhere around 20 additional visits spread over four months. If memory serves me correctly, we couldn't locate 4473 forms for several transactions, the Disposition side was also improperly filled out covering the sale of 4 Glock pistols to a local police department right up the road (we only listed the name of the Department but didn't have an official letter from the Chief acknowledging receipt of the guns) and we mixed up two transfers in the A&D book by listing each customer with the other customer's gun, even though the correct guns were listed on each 4473.

There were other errors, such as not spelling out the name of a county in a personal address and, in fact, that error occurred numerous times. Why?

Because most of our customers came from the two Massachusetts counties which surround the shop's location – Hampden and Hampshire Counties – and one of the kids who worked in the store would frequently enter the county as 'HAM' whenever a customer said that he didn't actually know the name of the county in which he lived. Now in fact the ATF could have made me call up every one of those customers and tell them to come into the shop and correct this important error, because under the rules, only the buyer can make changes to Section A, which are the fields for personal information which identifies the buyer, but I was let off the hook when it came to correcting this serious mistake. The fact that the 4473 form also contains a field for the buyer's zip code which is specific to one county or the other doesn't matter – the ATF examiner told me that any abbreviation is a 'serious' mistake.

On the other hand, where I really screwed up was on the Acquisition side of the A&D register, because the inspection turned up thousands of errors here, not hundreds mind you, but thousands, all of which should have been fixed. And what was this mistake? Remember that the ATF considers such mistakes as possibly leading to diverting guns into the illegal market, impeding the tracing of guns, and worst of all creating safety issues for the public. And

I had made this mistake *thousands* of times. Here was the mistake.

Over the thirteen years or so covered by this inspection, I had probably purchased 6,000 or 7,000 guns from a single source, namely, a wholesaler who was located about a thirty minutes' drive from my shop. I liked working with this company, I knew the staff well, they often would give me hard-to-get guns which could easily and quickly be sold, and I saved time and money by stopping off at their warehouse every couple of days to pick up merchandise rather than waiting around for the delivery via UPS.

This wholesaler had been in business for over 50 years, it was one of 30-odd national gun wholesalers operating in the entire United States and, in fact, the company had undergone their own ATF inspection the year before the same IOI gang showed up to audit me. So it wasn't as if I was getting the guns from some back-door dealer in Podunk, MO or from some FFL-holder who drove around here and there selling guns out of the trunk of his car. Probably 90% of my new gun inventory came from this one distributor, who couldn't have been better known to the ATF.

Every week I usually purchased 25-30 guns from this wholesaler and when I returned to the store the first thing I would do was enter the new inventory into the A&D. And the reason I did those entries within 5 minutes after walking into the shop was that one day I was unpacking the guns, a customer saw one that he just 'had to have,' he paid cash right on the spot, filled out a 4473, I made the call to the FBI and off he went. Now the good news is that I had added the details about the gun to the 4473 but it wasn't until several days had passed that I realized that the gun had never been listed on the A&D. It wasn't difficult to correct the mistake because I had both the customer's 4473 and the wholesale invoice, both of which listed the gun. But that experience taught me that we never finished a gun sale and let a gun leave the store until every gun received that day had been put into the A&D register so it could be properly tracked when and if it was then sold.

But time is also money in a retail business, so when I came into the shop with 25 guns, I wanted to get them into the A&D book as quickly as I could. So on the Acquisition side of the register where I was required to provide the source of the gun, I simply entered the name of the wholesaler on the first line of each page and then put hash marks for all the remaining lines on that page. What I was *supposed to do* for e very single entry was to write out the wholesaler's complete name and the complete number of the wholesaler's FFL. I didn't do this thousands of times which meant I made thousands of mistakes in my A&D book.

Now the reader is probably sitting there slightly bored, scratching his or her head and wondering why I am going into such detail about such silly and stupid bureaucratic mistakes. I'll tell you why. Because if I had chosen to continue my retail business after the ATF inspection ended, I would have been required to go to a meeting at ATF headquarters in Boston where all my mistakes would have been reviewed, I would have agreed that my work had been sloppy, I would have also promised to be a good boy and make sure to do things the correct way, and then I would have gone back and continued to operate my store. And by the way, in the four or more months between when the audit ended and all these mistakes had been found until the post-inspection meeting had actually taken place, I would have been allowed to continue running my gun shop and selling guns as if no audit had even taken place.

On the other hand, when the ATF finished inspecting Riverview following Sandy Hook, they didn't find thousands of errors, they didn't find hundreds of errors, they weren't looking for errors at all. They had already reviewed with Dave the result of their last Riverview inspection, everyone had agreed on the mistakes which were found, and the ATF was allegedly going to issue a report that would recommend a temporary, ninety-day shutdown to give Dave time to institute a better paperwork process and train store staff. None of that happened because the ATF had the authority to make up or change the rules as it went along. And once 26 people were murdered in Sandy Hook with a gun bought at Riverview, the rules as they were applied to Dave Laguercia would be drastically and immediately changed.

Two more points that need to be remembered as we go forward to relate Dave Laguercia's tale of woe. When my audit was finished the ATF inspectors and I agreed that I had been unable to produce paperwork on four guns. We had the manufacturer's name, the type of gun, the caliber, serial number and so forth but we could not produce the requisite paperwork to show for sure what happened to those weapons after they were brought into the store. And the inability of a dealer to account for inventory is, for obvious reasons, considered the most serious mistake of all.

Know what happened? I called a nice lady in the Atlanta ATF office who runs what is known as the 'missing and stolen' list, and gave her the information on each gun. Now in fact, in addition to the error of not having the paperwork, I had also committed a serious felony because the law requires that a dealer notify the 'missing and stolen' lady within 48 hours after the gun disappears. I hadn't done that with any of these four guns. I also hadn't informed the local police department about these missing guns, which is also a felony in my state. Which means I could have been facing 40 years in jail. By the way, I've never even visited a jail, either before or after my inspection by the ATF.

The other thing you need to remember for later reference is that over the years the ATF contacted me perhaps two or three times each year and asked me to respond to a trace. What this meant is that I had been identified as the dealer who sold a gun to someone and now that particular gun had become the subject of some kind of official concern. I never received a trace request that I didn't answer within the time allotted for such things which is normally 24 hours although the ATF is flexible because sometimes a trace request would roll in on a day that the shop was closed. Nevertheless, to the extent possible I always tried to help prevent a crime by responding to traces right away. According to what the ATF blithely refers to as a 'Fact Sheet' on tracing, "its purpose is to provide investigative leads in the fight against violent crime and terrorism and to enhance public safety."[10]

In fact, when law enforcement agencies request a trace to be conducted by the ATF, they must specify the reason for the trace from one or a combination of 64 different categories. Since there is no category covering anything having to do with terrorism, we can ignore the ATF's claim that the National Tracing Center provides investigative leads in that area. As for the fight against violent crime, less than 20% of all gun traces involve guns that were picked up during the investigation of a serious crime; i.e., homicide, aggravated assault, robbery, etc. The number one category for tracing is for something called 'firearm under investigation,' but this doesn't necessarily reflect the commission or investigation of any crime at all. Many LE agencies are required to get trace information for any unclaimed gun that is found within their jurisdiction, including the rusted old guns found in Grandpa's basement after he's carted off to the undertaker or a rest home; agencies may do a trace for a gun that is reported missing, whether the person who initiates the report knows why the gun is missing or not. More than 20,000 traces each year are for 'found firearm,' which is often nothing more than a gun that turns up in the trash, or under the seat of an abandoned car.[11]

The point here is that the ATF wants the public to believe that the money the agency spends on regulating dealers, which includes tracing activities, is somehow making the public safer and protecting us from crime. In fact, the agency often refers to every gun it traces as a 'crime gun,' as if the 300,000+ traces they run each year have helped solve 300,000+ crimes. And this image, carefully nurtured in press release after release, is what made the public believe that Dave Laguercia was a threat to public safety, because otherwise why was it necessary following Sandy Hook for the ATF to storm his shop?

I once received an ATF trace request on an individual who bought a gun in my shop and then moved to Florida. Now a Florida resident, this person had been arrested for something or other and at the time of his arrest had been carrying the gun he purchased from me. Within 24 hours after I received the trace request I had located the 4473, faxed it to the ATF and figured that was the end of that. Several days later an ATF agent from the IOI division came into my shop and told me he needed to look at the actual 4473 form to make sure I had faxed the original one to the tracing center because it turned out that the individual who had been arrested in Florida was identified as a man whereas my 4473 form had the gender box for 'female' checked and the discrepancy needed to be cleared up. It turned out, and this is the God's honest truth, that it was finally determined that the woman who had purchased the gun in my shop had undergone a sex-change operation at some later date and was now a man.

One more quick ATF story and we'll move on. One day during the inspection of my gun shop, the leader of the IOI team asked me to give him and his colleagues a tour of the entire store. Now in fact I wasn't required to do so since I had already given them the documentation to which they were entitled to see, and without a search warrant, from a legal point of view, I didn't have to show them around. Moreover, they couldn't have produced a search warrant because the IOI staff are basically high-priced clerks without any law enforcement duties or authority at all. But I'm actually very proud of the interior of my building which, in addition to the retail area, also has a large conference center, a classroom and a private shooting range.

At one point during the tour we happened to walk through the classroom and sitting on the table was the frame of a shotgun without any barrel or stock and in fact, the frame didn't contain any movable parts (hammer, trigger, bolt) of any kind. But the frame did have a serial number which, believe it or not, made this empty piece of metal, legally speaking, a gun. The IOI team leader grabbed the frame, hoisted it over his head like a golfer might show off the Master's trophy he had just won and yelled out to everyone, "Hey – here's another gun!"

I don't recall whether in the final inspection report this IOI bunch stated that as a result of their investigation an unlisted gun turned up, but as soon as we all returned to the retail area I was instructed with great solemnity to list the gun in the A&D. Which I did. I couldn't put down a caliber because the gun didn't have a barrel and where there was a space to list the gun's source, I wrote 'ATF.'

A week after the ATF finished their audit I decided to close the retail operation in the store. This decision was largely due to the fact that I had just been told that the two young brothers who actually ran the store had just been offered full-time law enforcement gigs and I didn't want to go through the hassle of hiring someone I didn't know and might not be able to trust. Moreover, I had begun developing a very active business as a gun trainer and journalist, which not only brought in a nice chunk of dough every week but kept me out of the clutches both of the Massachusetts Department of Revenue and the ATF.

After I made the decision to stop selling retail guns, I surrendered my FFL. The IOI team from the ATF then actually showed up, packed up all my 4473 forms of which there were more than 12,000 and paid to have them shipped down to the warehouse in West Virginia. I assume they are now rotting in one of the trailers now being used to store paperwork because the ATF warehouse has no more room. What pleases me more than anything is that the last gun I put into my inventory was a gun that came from the ATF.

And talking about guns, it's now time to have a serious discussion in Chapter 3 about a particular gun, the gun which Nancy Lanza purchased from Dave Laguercia which her son Adam took with him when he drove to the elementary school in Sandy Hook.

CHAPTER 3

A GUN

On August 1, 1966, a 25-year old ex-Marine named Charles Whitman went up to the observation deck on the campus of the University of Texas at Austin, and over the next hour and a half killed 11 people and wounded 31 more.[1] Before he began firing from the tower, he had already killed his mother in her house the night before, killed his wife in their house the next morning before setting out for the campus, killed three more people within the tower building before going up to the top, then set up his arsenal and began blazing away.

This incident was considered the first mass shooting in contemporary times and Whitman would continue to hold the dubious record for the highest number of killings in one location until Seung-Hui Cho went on his spree at the Virginia Tech Campus in 2007. Like the other mass shooters whose behavior is briefly covered in Chapter 1, Whitman had not been considered a risk to himself or anyone else in the period leading up to his fatal attack. He also had obviously been planning some kind of shooting incident for some time. And like the other mass shooters, with the exception of James Holmes, Whitman did not survive the event. Hence, much of what we believe about how Whitman changed from being a seemingly 'normal' person to a ghastly mass murderer is nothing more than theories based on little or no real facts.

The one fact about Charles Whitman that we do know however, is what kind of gun he used to commit his deadly acts. And while this might seem to be a rather inconsequential piece of evidence by which to compare Whitman's behavior to the behavior of other mass murderers who seem to pop up in America with a stunning degree of regularity that happens nowhere else, understanding the weapon that Whitman used and how he used it tells us a great deal not only about him, but about the other mass murders which occurred between when Whitman climbed up the Texas Tower and Adam Lanza's entrance into the Sandy Hook school.

Before I go further into the issue of Whitman's choice and use of guns, I want to first make a brief detour to cover in a somewhat abstract way some gun nomenclature that readers need to understand in order to properly evaluate the issues involved in mass shooting events. In talking about how guns are designed and how they work, I promise to make this as simple and easy to understand as I can.

A gun is a mechanical device which pushes a solid object in the direction intended by the operator of the device. The very first guns appeared somewhere during the 13th century in China, and they consisted of a long, metal tube into which was put gunpowder and on top of the gunpowder was placed a solid, metal ball which would fly out of the barrel due to the force and expanding gas pressures created by the explosion of the gunpowder. This device was called a cannon.

Over the next century, cannons were made smaller and much lighter, such devices were called rifles, and when they were made even smaller and even more lighter, they were called handguns. But whether the device weighed several hundred pounds, had a barrel length of 4 or 5 feet, a barrel diameter of a foot and fired a round ball which might travel several hundred yards, or whether it was a device which weighed less than a pound, had a barrel length of 12 inches, a barrel diameter of less than an inch and fired a round ball that weighed an ounce or less, the principle and design was exactly the same: in order for any gun to work regardless of size, it has to be loaded with a charge, or what is called a propellant, and it also needs a solid object which will travel away from the device, and this is referred to as the ball, or the bullet or the shell.

In the seven centuries or so since the Chinese invented the first gun, the basic design has been modified and refined, but not really changed. The two major refinements were in the manner in which the ammunition was placed into the barrel, and the way in which the propellant or charge ignites, creating the pressures which then forces the ammunition out of the gun. Like most gun technologies, these developments came about to satisfy the requirements of the military, since it was obviously the armies which had the greatest need for weapons that would give them more firepower in the event of a war.

The first great change was in the design of the ammunition which initially was loaded into the gun by ramming a packet of powder down the barrel and following that with a ball. In the 1840s, this process started to be replaced by the invention of the cartridge, a cylindrical metal case which held both the powder and the bullet. The cartridge also contained a small metal component called a primer, chemicals that when struck on the outside with a metal pin (the 'firing' pin) produce a spark which ignites the powder and up the barrel flies the shell. Adding the primer to the cartridge meant that the process of igniting the powder was no longer a separate operation from the process then needed to fire the gun. Cock the hammer, pull the trigger, hammer drops on firing pin and – *bam!*

By the end of the American Civil War, every modern army was carrying breech-loading as opposed to barrel-loading guns, and these gun products, along with the ammunition they used were also getting into civilian hands. But the equally important design change which allowed the entire process of loading the guns to be automated through the pressures and gases released by the ignition of the propellant appeared first in Germany near the end of the nineteenth century, but was then incorporated into shotgun, handgun and rifle designs by a remarkable American gun inventor named John Browning, whose advances in design basically revolutionized the entire field of military and civilian small arms.

Browning figured out how to use the gases and pressures created by the detonation of the gunpowder to make two things happen: first, and this was not anything particularly new, he used the pressures to propel the bullet out of the barrel. But more important, he also figured out how to design guns so that at the same time the bullet was going forward through the barrel, the bolt would move backwards, eject the empty cartridge and push a new, unfired cartridge into place. What this meant was that the entire process of loading ammunition into a gun every time it was fired was now no longer manually performed by the gun operator, but by the action of the gun itself due to the pressures released by the ignition of the shell.

Once Browning figured out the mechanics which automated the loading of ammunition, he then also figured out how to design small arms so that the action of the hammer falling on the firing pin and pushing it into the primer required a pull on the trigger for each shot, or the loading process could be repeated again and again with only one trigger pull until the ammunition ran out. The latter process became known as automatic fire, the former known as semi-automatic fire. Now that we understand the basic nomenclature of how guns work, let's return to our discussion about how these mass shootings got started when Charlie Whitman went up to the top of the Texas Tower and began to aim and shoot at every human being in sight.

Prior to being gunned down by the cops, Whitman killed and wounded 44 people from his perch slightly less than 300 feet above the campus below. The time involved from the first shot he fired until his life came to an end was roughly 90 minutes, and he may have fired as many as 100 rounds, even though the exact count of shell casings found near his body was never released. He also shot randomly while people on the ground even returned some fire (this was Texas after all) with students as far as 500 yards from the tower being hit.

The gun Whitman used was a Remington Model 700 bolt-action rifle, chambered in 6mm Remington cartridge with a 4-power scope. The 6mm Remington cartridge was originally a 24-caliber round but fell by the wayside as hunters began switching to the .243 Winchester, which was a high-powered, more powerful round but delivered tolerable recoil, making it a good 'starter' cartridge for younger boys and women who wanted to hunt. The good news about the 6mm is that with a 100-grain bullet weight, the round chucked along at more than 2,500 feet per second out of the barrel, and unless it was a very windy day, would only drop five or six inches over the first 300 yards.

The Remington 700 rifle is probably the best-selling, standard hunting rifle of all time, and even though there has been a consistent difficulty with the safety which has embroiled the gun maker in a class action suit for more than 20 years, by and large the gun holds up well.[2] For many years I owned a Remington 700 in 270 Winchester, a classic deer caliber, the 6mm being perhaps just a tad light for deer kills unless you hit the exact, lethal spot. Whitman had qualified as a Marine Corps marksman which meant that using this gun with a 4-power scope would certainly have been enough weapon to hit just about anything he could see.

On the other hand, the rifle's capacity was 5 rounds, one in the breech and the other 4 in the magazine which had to be loaded round by round by springing open the bolt and manually pulling it all the way back to the cheek piece of the stock. In other words, what Whitman gained in accuracy, which allowed him to play sniper from the top of a 300-foor tower, he lost in the time required to reload the gun between each shot as well as inserting fresh ammunition every fourth or fifth round. And although he carried a whole arsenal of weapons up to the top of the tower, including an M-1 carbine, a Remington pump-action 35-caliber rifle, a semi-auto shotgun and two handguns, the only weapon he could use to reach targets on the ground was a bolt-action, manually fed gun.

Whitman was the first and last mass shooter, from then until now, who committed his rampage with a weapon that did not automatically reload after every shot. And this was obviously because he knew that his position in the tower gave him time enough to murder a lot of people even though his rate of fire would have been very slow. Indeed, what he needed to use was a weapon that had a premium on long-distance accuracy rather than speed or ease of use.

Every gun that was the primary weapon of rampage shooters like Klebold and Harris, Seung-Hui Cho, James Holmes, Elliott Rodger and Adam Lanza was a magazine-fed, high-capacity handgun or long gun that could deliver 15 or more rounds prior to reloading and then could be reloaded with a fresh, hi-capacity magazine in two seconds or less. And it is the design of such weapons which has become the major bone of contention between gun rights versus gun control advocates every time a mass shooting provokes a public gun debate.

Prior to leaving his house in Sandy Hook, getting in his car and driving over to the school, Adam Lanza shot and killed his mother who was still asleep in her bed. He killed her with a rifle, but it wasn't the rifle he used to slaughter 26 people inside the school. For that ten-minute exercise in mass mayhem he used a Bushmaster XM-15 assault rifle which could load and fire 30-rounds of extremely lethal military ammunition within a minute or less.

Adan Lanza shot his mother with 4 rounds from a bolt-action, 22-caliber rifle, the Savage Mark II. This gun, often called a 'first gun,' is frequently the type of weapon purchased for a young person who is just getting into guns. Because it takes a 22LR shell, it has little recoil and therefore easily controlled by a new or young shooter. The caliber is certainly lethal, but nowhere as dangerous as the .223 caliber that loads into the Bushmaster XM-15. Most important is the fact that after shooting the gun each time, the shooter has to manually work the bolt, eject the spent cartridge and load a fresh round into the breech of the gun.

Had Adam Lanza taken the Savage Mark II rifle to Sandy Hook school, he may not have even been able to get into the building, since the 22LR caliber might not have been powerful enough to break the glass panels (which he shot out with the XM-15) and allow him entrance into the school. And even if he had gained access to the interior, the bolt design of the Mark II would have made it virtually impossible for him to inflict anywhere near the degree of damage that he was able to deliver with the Bushmaster XM-15.

Let's assume for a moment that the Ochberg-Fusilier diagnosis of rampage shooters is valid and that until the morning of December 14, 2012, nobody could have predicted that Adam Lanza would suddenly manifest a psychopathic disorder and begin killing everyone he could. The fact is that without access to the XM-15 Bushmaster rifle, it would have been impossible for him to have murdered more than several people, in other words, he might not have ended up being a mass murderer at all.

What the 'threat assessment perspective' authored by authorities like Ochberg and Fuselier after Columbine said about access to guns not being a significant factor in explaining acts of mass murder simply wasn't accurate because what was not understood by these experts was that it wasn't a question of access to any kind of gun, but access to the *particular* type of gun that Nancy Lanza bought from Dave LaGuercia.

This is what needs to be understood about all mass shootings, namely, that psychopaths or not, rampage shooters usually choose exactly the type of weapon that will be most effective and efficient weapon for the type of shooting rampage they plan to commit. The rifle which Charles Whitman used to kill and injure scores of people would have created minimal damage if James Holmes had carried it into the Century 16 where he killed and injured 82 theater-goers who thought they were just going to see the latest Batman movie until the smoke bombs went off and Holmes opened up. Which is why we need to understand why certain kinds of guns are for mass shooters, the weapons of choice.

On July 1, 1993, a 55-year old self-employed businessman, Gian Ferri, walked into a law firm in the middle of downtown San Francisco and began shooting the place up.[3] He ended up killing 8 and wounding 6 others, then took his own life. Ferri walked into the law firm with an Intratec 9, which was also the gun used by Klebold and Harris at Columbine High. The Tec-9, as it is called, looks like a machine pistol; i.e., a military-style handgun which can be operated in fully-automatic mode, but as a gun for the civilian market, the Tec-9 is sold only as a semi-auto weapon but uses a high-capacity mag.

The result of this shooting was an 'assault-weapon' ban passed in California and then copied by the Clinton Administration in 1994.[4] Basically, the law prohibited for ten years the manufacture of guns which were called 'assault weapons' if their design included certain military-style features that were found on variations of the military rifle known as the M-16. The guns had to use detachable magazines along with at least two other design features, including folding stocks, pistol grips, bayonet mounts or flash suppressor – any rifle or handguns with two such features plus a detachable magazine was considered an 'assault weapon' and therefore prohibited from being made or being sold.

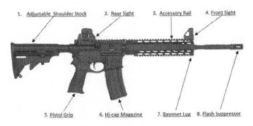

Figure 3. AR-15 showing gun parts #1, 5-8 that were prohibited by 1994 ban.

In addition to prohibiting certain design features, the law also prohibited the manufacture of long gun or handgun magazines with capacities of more than 10 rounds. Which meant that most of the new, European-based pistols made by companies like Beretta, Sig and Glock could no longer be sold with what were called 'double-stack' magazines which held 15 or more rounds. Actually, this part of the law had the unintended (or maybe intended) benefit of making the older-style, single-action American pistols like the Colt 1911 more competitive, because these guns had never used magazines which held more than 7 or 8 rounds and such guns had been largely squeezed out of the market when the hi-cap, European handguns began to appear.

The assault weapons ban exempted law enforcement guns from the design prohibitions and also exempted police handguns from the high-capacity ban, as well as not restricting commercial sale of guns with these features that had been manufactured prior to the date the law took effect. Nevertheless, the law was seen as a significant threat against gun 'rights' because for the first time since the National Firearms Act (NFA) passed in 1934, the government was setting design standards for what kinds of weapons civilians could and couldn't own.[5]

The gun industry didn't voice any strong objections to the NFA because everyone agreed that machine guns, like the type of weapon used by the Al Capone gang in the St. Valentine's Day massacre, were too lethal to fall into citizen's hands. But the NFA did allow for civilian ownership of fully-automatic weapons provided the purchaser first underwent a detailed legal vetting and background check, whereas the 1994 law simply said that this and that type of gun could no longer be sold at all.

When the assault weapons ban expired in 2004, with the exception of what pro-gun folks refer to as the 'Communist' states like Massachusetts and California which opted to continue the ban, military-style rifles and hi-capacity handgun and long gun magazines once again were made available for civilian sale. And the reappearance of these products coincided with a general easing of concealed-carry restrictions which created a greater demand for the types of weapons that the 1994 law had previously banned.

It also created the development of a myth about the weapon of choice for most rampage shootings, the military-style rifles like the AR-15 and the AK-47, which have been promoted by the gun industry as 'sporting arms' rather than 'assault weapons' in an effort to shield the industry from the possibility of additional restrictions that always loom whenever a mass shooting occurs. The emotional response to mass shootings is not a function of the number of victims created by the shooting incident per se, but rather the degree of attention paid to such events by the media. Whitman's rampage in Texas, for example, was considered the second most-covered media story of 1966, second only to coverage of the Viet Nam War.[6] Lanza's frenzy was and remains a focus of media concern. And the wave of emotion which breaks out in the wake of a mass shooting could always generate more regulatory problems for gun makers and gun sellers.

Given the unpredictability of the political response to mass shootings, the industry began to create a narrative about weapons like the AR-15 and AK-47 that describes them as no different from any other kind of semi-automatic weapon never having been considered as being more lethal or dangerous than any other kind of small arm whose ownership is, after all, protected as a Constitutional 'right.' And since semi-automatic long guns and hand guns have been part of the civilian arsenal since they were first developed and introduced, as long as gun makers can differentiate these weapons from 'weapons of war,' they should remain within the boundaries of what is considered a legal firearm that can be owned by any law-abiding citizen.

This strategy, which is nothing other than a marketing ploy, is based on the idea that as long as a gun can only be fired in semi-automatic fashions; i.e., every shot requires a separate pull of the trigger, the gun should therefore be considered a 'sporting' gun whose sale and use should not be regulated in any way other than the regulations that cover all commercially-available guns.[7] And since military rifles have been designed to deliver full-auto performance, and since everyone has accepted the strict regulation of full-auto weapons since 1934, there is no reason to restrict the sale and ownership of AR-15 or AK-47 rifles in the same way that we do not enforce special restrictions on any other type of semi-automatic small arm, nor do we still restrict the magazine capacity of semi-automatic guns following the sunset of the 1994 assault weapons ban in 2004.

The problem with this argument, however, is that it flies in the face of both historical facts and the reason why assault-style long guns and hi-capacity handguns are invariably used by people who commit mass murders, even when those events do not result in the horrifyingly death toll that came out of Aurora, Columbine or Sandy Hook. The FBI defines a mass shooting as any event in which 4 persons are killed or wounded in the same location by the same shooter or shooters at one time.[8] The list also includes shootings in which the shooter turns the gun on himself. In 2016 there were at least 375 such shootings, which left more than 1,000 persons dead other than the shooter - roughly the same number occurred again in 2015.[9] Which means that these events account for at least 10% of all gun homicides each year.

Although it would be impossible to determine how many of these mass shootings were perpetrated by shooters whose guns contained hi-cap mags, to the extent that most pistols today contain hi-cap mags, it is reasonable to assume that notwithstanding the idea promoted by pro-gun advocates that hi-cap mags are just another, modern adaptation of traditional gun technologies, in fact, it is indisputable that there exists is a link between the number of rounds that a gun can be fired without needing to be reloaded and the ease and speed with which multiple victims can be gunned down.

What the gun industry has tried to do to avoid the legal threats which would ensue with a continued spate of mass killings is to promote the idea that the AR-15, because it can only be loaded and shot in semi-auto mode, is therefore a 'modern sporting rifle,' which is no different from any other type of semi-auto long gun. And while there is a measure of truth to this argument, like all arguments which are based only on a partial truth, a more honest approach to the issue of how and why such guns turn up again and again in mass shootings shows that the 'sporting rifle' concept as a means of protecting the gun industry from a backlash created by a mass shooting event is basically made up of whole cloth.

First, the distinction between 'sporting' guns and military guns as being based only on whether the gun can fire semi-auto or full-auto is simply not true. The current military gun carried by U.S. forces, the M4 rifle, is manufactured as a 'selective-fire' gun, which means that the shooter can manually switch the gun back and forth from semi to full-auto mode. This design feature is found on the M4 to give the trooper more flexibility in being able to adjust how the gun will be used depending on the specific tactical situation; some live-fire conditions are better served if the operator can deliver multiple rounds with one trigger pull, other situations, particularly when long-distance accuracy is essential, are better met in semi-auto mode. To pretend that every semi-auto gun is, by definition, a sporting weapon would therefore presume that when a soldier in a battle zone adjusts his M4 to fire as a semi-auto weapon that he (or she) is now going into battle with a sporting gun. Which of course is not the case at all.

Second and more important is that what makes the M4 a 'weapon of war' is not just whether it fires in full-auto mode, but the way in which the gun loads and is deployed by the shooter when it is being used. What distinguishes the military rifle from civilian semi-auto hunting or target rifles is the fact that the M-4 or AR-15 magazine loads into the gun from below the stock, which not only makes it much quicker to drop an empty magazine and replace it with a fresh magazine that contains a full complement of rounds, but a bottom-loaded magazine can hold many more rounds than if it loaded from the top of the stock which would limit its capacity to only 4 or 5 rounds.

Finally, and here is the reason why an assault-style or what is often referred to as a tactical rifle should not be considered as a sporting gun. The whole point of the tactical design is to give the shooter a much higher degree of physical mobility while, at the same time, not compromising how quickly and efficiently he can use the gun. In every single shooting rampage since Whitman, the extreme toll of dead and injured reflected most of all the ability of the shooter to move around in an enclosed area that contained a crowd of people while aiming and shooting the gun at the same time.

This shooting technique, which requires the shooter to quickly acquire the target area while he is also moving about is more commonly used with handguns because they are small, light and therefore easily shifted from one target to another even if neither the shooter or the targets are standing still. On the other hand, mobile shooting is particularly difficult with most sporting rifles because of the stock design and the manner in which the gun has to be reloaded every several rounds. These problems are eliminated with the AR design, which is why shooters like Adam Lanza and James Holmes were able to move quickly from one spot to another while touching off multiple rounds, thus creating a much higher victim count before they were done.

The weapon of choice for some mass shooters has been the semi-auto version of Mikhail Kalashnikov's rifle design, the AK-47. The gun industry has not spent as much time or effort talking about this weapon as a 'modern sporting rifle' because the rifle is often carried and pictured in the hands of terrorist bad guys and the industry is not entirely comfortable talking about the American 'tradition' of sporting rifles when every day on television we see the AK being brandished about by ISIS fighters or other terrorist groups. It is also why AK-47 rifles are manufactured only in small quantities within the United States, but the reasons the gun is so popular outside our borders is exactly the same reasons as why the AR-15 is so popular over here. Simply put – neither of these guns were designed for anything except as weapons that could be used to kill human beings, which is why the idea that David Laguercia sold a 'modern sporting rifle' to Nancy Lanza is just so much talk.

Before Nancy Lanza bought the AR-15 at Riverview Sales she also bought a Sig P226. This handgun holds 15 rounds of lethal, 9mm ammunition, it was the gun that Heung-Sui Cho used to mow down 49 people and then used on himself at Virginia Tech; it was also the same gun which Elliott Rodger carried as he careened around Isla Vista and killed or wounded 10 people besides himself. Had Nancy Lanza purchased only the Sig pistol from Riverview and acquired the AR rifle somewhere else, we still might be telling what happened to a gun dealer after Sandy Hook, but the dealer would have been someone other than Dave.

Recall in the previous chapter that we covered an incident in 2010 when Laguercia was mistakenly identified as the dealer who sold a pistol to Omar Thornton, who then went down to a Budweiser wholesaler, shot and killed 8 people, wounded 2 more and then turned the gun on himself. Not only did the ATF not even bother to show up at Riverside Sales on that occasion, they never even contacted Dave after that event, even though two years later following Sandy Hook the media mistakenly claimed that Riverview also sold the weapon used by Thornton, thus burnishing Laguercia's reputation as a master seller of mass murder guns.

To understand why the gun used by Adam Lanza plays such an important in the whole issue of mass shootings we need to make one more assumption about what actually took place on December 14, 2012. Had Adam Lanza survived the rampage and been arrested the way that James Holmes was taken into custody while standing outside of the Century 16, he would have been charged with multiple murders as well as violations of two firearms laws. One law prohibited anyone under 21 years old from possessing a handgun and Lanza drove to the elementary school with both a Gig and a Glock. He would also have been in violation of a second law passed under the Poppa Bush Administration, which made it a federal offense to bring a gun onto the property of a K-12 school.

This law, known as the Gun-Free School Zones Act, was initially passed in 1990, then struck down by the Supreme Court in 1995, amended and slipped back into an appropriation bill by the Clinton Administration and has been on the books ever since.[10] The law basically prohibits carrying a loaded, concealed weapon onto any public or private K-12 educational facility, unless the individual is either law enforcement or has a concealed-carry license issued by the state of residence of the individual who brings the gun onto school grounds.

Lanza would have also been charged with violating a second and federal gun offense, namely, being in possession of a handgun even though he was not yet 21. Had he been in the company of his mother, the legal owner of the Sig and the Glock handguns that he also brought into the school, he would not have violated this statute because it could be presumed that the proximity of his mother would make her the custodian of the weapons and therefore responsible for his behavior with said guns. Bu because she was not with him when he shot his way into the front hallway of the school by dint of the fact that she was at home with four bullets in her head, meant that he was not legally allowed to be carrying the handguns onto school property or anywhere else.

Why do I raise this seemingly innocuous legal issue? Because from the time Adam Lanza left his house at 36 Yogananda Street and drove the five miles to the elementary school, had he only taken the AR rifle into his car, he would have been in violation of no gun law at all. In fact, he had a state-issued gun license which enabled him to transport both the AR and the ammunition used by the gun. And since there was no legal limit on the amount of ammunition he could carry along with the gun, he was not breaking any law by transporting the more than 90 rounds that he fired off within the school. Had Lanza, like Holmes, targeted a movie theater instead of a school, he would not have broken any federal or state law by using the most lethal weapon that could be legally owned by any 18-year old never charged with a serious crime.

Not only was Adam Lanza not breaking any laws by carrying around an AR-15, in fact he had been encouraged in such behavior by his parents from his early youth, having been taken for recreational shooting at public ranges from the age of five. His father never purchased guns for Adam, but was aware that Nancy Lanza was supplying their son with guns and ammunition, and despite the fact that both parents showed endless concern for Adam's mental state, and both noted a deteriorating mental situation in their son during the period leading up to the rampage, there is no evidence that either parent considered Adam's access to guns as a risk or a threat to himself or anyone else.

The fact that Adam shot his mother with a 22-caliber, bolt-action rifle on the morning of December 14, 2002, but then left that gun in the house and carried the AR to the elementary school indicates that he certainly understood the degree to which the AR rifle could be used to inflict a degree of damage that could not have occurred had he taken the Savage Mark II rifle to the school. Or, for that matter, *had he not been able to get his hands on an AR-15 at all.* Anyone who thinks for one moment that both the Savage Mark II and the Smith & Wesson AR-15 were just two types of 'modern sporting rifles' is as delusional about the difference between these two weapons as Adam Lanza's parents were delusional about the fact that their son's unquestioned access to the AR-15 was not something which needed to be prevented or at least monitored and controlled.

In the report by the Office of Child Advocate released the year following the Sandy Hook massacre, the report's authors, all of whom were professional experts in the fields of mental health and child advocacy, listed 37 'key findings' from their year's work, including Adam's "significant developmental challenges from earliest childhood," the degree to which special educational services were "limited," the extent to which he was "profoundly impaired by anxiety and Obsessive-Compulsive Disorder" and the fact that "minimal mental health evaluation and treatment was obtained."[11] None of these factors, however, constituted a "direct line of causation" to the events that took place at Sandy Hook.

On the other hand, the report also notes as a key finding that Adam "retained access to numerous firearms and high capacity ammunition magazines even as his mental health deteriorated in late adolescence," which "cannot be ignored as a critical factor in this tragedy." But not ignoring something is very different from assigning primary cause. And just as the experts who studied Columbine and found that it was mistaken media coverage which assigned primary responsibility for the rampage to the ease at which Klebold and Harris could get their hands on hi-capacity, semi-automatic guns, so the experts who weighed in on why Adam Lanza committed his assault also could not bring themselves to understand the fundamental importance of Lanza's ability to get his hands on an AR-15.

Without the existence of the AR-15 in the Lanza household, Sandy Hook would not have occurred. And since neither Adam Lanza nor his mother could be held legally responsible for the existence of this gun, the authorities demonstrated that they were doing something to bring some measure of justice to the victims and their community by working their way back up the supply chain and landing on Dave Laguercia as he was going about his usual business at Riverside Sales.

CHAPTER 4

THE BLAME GAME BEGINS

On Friday, December 14, 2012, Julie Bannerman returned from lunch to her desk at the New York advertising agency where she was an account exec.[1] As she sat down, she flicked on her computer monitor which was always set to the CNN website in case there might be a breaking story which involved one of her clients, her portfolio being anchored by several national brands. As the monitor came into focus she also punched a code into her desk phone because the message light was blinking which meant that calls had come in while she had been out.

As she listened to the first message, which was from her sister telling her in no uncertain tones to 'call back,' her eyes focused on the CNN website where the Breaking News caption at the bottom of the screen read: *Shooting at Connecticut Elementary School; at least 3 victims at hospital; condition 'very serious,'* and then below the headline a scrolling message about Senator John Kerry being considered for Secretary of State.

Since her computer audio was muted, Julie couldn't hear what was being said by what appeared to be a young school child who was responding to a reporter's question outside the school.

The fact that there had been a school shooting which appeared to have injured several people was hardly news to Julie Bannerman who was old enough to remember where she was when she first heard about the assassination of President Kennedy in 1963. But just as she was about to flick off her browser and go into her email account, another agency employee came up to her desk and said, "Did you hear what just happened in Newtown?"

To which Julie said something like, "Yea, a couple of people have been shot at some school," and her colleague shook her head and replied in a very emotional voice: "No, no, that's not true! They shot lots of kids, there are dead kids in every room. It's a slaughter." And as the other woman began backing away from Julie's desk, her hands pressed against both sides of her head, Julie reopened her browser, turned up the audio volume and began what would become a marathon of viewing computers and television sets for millions of Americans throughout the land.

As part of the research for this book I spoke to several dozen people in locations throughout the

United States. I asked them three questions: 1). When did they first learn about Sandy Hook? 2) Where were they when they first got the news? 3) What, if they could recall, were their immediate thoughts? The responses I received should obviously not be viewed in any way as an exercise in scientific polling, but taken together, the answers reminded me of conversations I had with many people about the day of the World Trade Center attack.

In my own case, for example, I learned about 9-11 while eating breakfast in a diner located down the street from my gun shop which had a television tuned to the reports coming out of New York. As soon as I saw the reports I rushed home because there were at least 5 people, including my daughter and sister, who lived and worked in Manhattan, both literally a stone's throw away from the towers which were just crumbling down. I couldn't reach anyone by phone throughout the entire day, but by mid-afternoon I was able to make contact with everyone via email, and as soon as I knew that everyone near and dear to me was safe, I could then begin to follow events with a certain degree of detachment but certainly without calm.

Regarding the massacre at Sandy Hook, I didn't know anyone who lived in or near Newtown, so I was not emotionally involved anywhere near the degree to which I had been literally terrified when I saw the Twin Towers come down. But I knew where Newton was located, I drove past the community on a regular basis every time I went to New York City, and the fact that I was a gun dealer meant that any mass shooting would be of concern, particularly a shooting in which most of the victims were 6-year old kids.

All the people I talked to regarding their initial reaction to Sandy Hook, no matter where they lived, remembered exactly where they were when they heard the first reports either from watching media or conversations with friends, and in every single instance what stuck out in their minds was the fact that the assault took place in a primary school and the victims were first-graders, this detail being the most wrenching of all. Many of the people with whom I spoke recalled other mass shootings, but were often vague on details, in particular the locations where the shootings took place, the dates of the shootings, and the degree to which they continued to think about a particular shooting rampage after relevant news stories disappeared. But everyone, no matter where they lived, remembered Sandy Hook, up to and including the shooter's name.

Dave Laguercia learned about Newtown while he was browsing through the internet after he opened his store. As soon as he heard Lanza's name for the first time, he went into his digital A&D file, did a search keying purchaser's last name, and immediately realized that his store had sold the Sig 226 pistol to Nancy Lanza in 2010 and sold her the AR-15 rifle the following year. The moment he saw her name in his register, Dave knew there was going to be trouble ahead, because by this time the news reports, which had initially stated only several casualties were revising the victim count upward and it was going to be bad.

In his attempt to remember the exact chronology of events that day, as you can imagine it's not something all that easy for Dave to exactly sort out, he believes that he did his A&D search after he received a telephone call from an ATF agent wanting to verify that, in fact, Riverview had been the source of the Sig. Dave's wife Randi recalls it differently, believing that first Dave found both transfer listings and then took the ATF call. Either way, Dave and Randi agree that the ATF asked only about the sale of the Sig pistol, and it was Dave, who in responding to the trace call, also told them about the subsequent purchase of the AR-15.

In the same way that I closed my gun shop sometime on the afternoon of December 14, Dave Laguercia also closed up and went home early that day. But although we did exactly the same thing, our reasons were not the same at all. I closed my shop simply because I was sick and disgusted and didn't want to stick around. Dave closed his shop because by mid-afternoon he was receiving inquiries and visits from the media and the press.

I also received media calls while I was still in my shop, but the media representatives who contacted me were looking for some general quotes about guns and gun violence that they could run during the Newtown segment in the evening news reports. Two nights later, in fact, I even made a brief appearance on one of the MS-NBC night-time talk shows and when I asked the producer why they had picked me, he answered, "You're the only gun dealer we could find who doesn't rant about 2nd Amendment 'rights.'"

Dave Laguercia's new-found celebrity status with the media, of course, had nothing to do with his views on gun 'rights.' Someone had obviously leaked the source of the guns connected to the rampage to the purchase of those weapons at Riverview Sales. Ironically, had Dave's A&D register not been a state-of-the-art electronic program which allowed him to search by using any field in an A&D listing (I would never have been able to find such information in my A&D book because I still entered all the required information by hand) he might have only confirmed the sale of the Sig 226 pistol to Nancy Lanza, which was the only gun of the three brought into the building by Adam Lanza that he did not actually use.

Dave didn't open his shop again until the following Wednesday, simply because he drove by the store multiple times each day and saw reporters and television crews sitting around the parking lot in front of his door. He did, however, go into the shop through the rear entrance on Sunday afternoon, because he received another call from the ATF on Sunday morning, and they wanted to come by the store and pick up the two 4473 background-check forms filled out by Nancy Lanza covering purchases of the AR-15 and the Sig. The transfer of the two forms to ATF custody only required the time which Dave needed to make copies of the paperwork; nevertheless the meeting carried on for forty minutes or slightly more.

That the ATF agents came to the shop to collect the 4473 forms created in Dave what Hunter Thompson would call a feeling of 'fear and loathing,' fear because this was simply not the usual way in which ATF conducted a search, loathing because, from that moment on, Dave Laguercia and the government were on opposite and basically opposing sides. Given his typical sales volume, responding to an ATF search was not an uncommon thing at Riverview – you received a fax containing the manufacturer and serial number of the gun, the name of the source of the gun (factory, wholesaler, other dealer) and the date the previous possessor of the gun shipped it to you. And since the entries in the A&D register are kept in chronological order, assuming that you actually received that gun, just flip to the entries for that relevant date, grab the corresponding 4473, copy the form and fax it back to the ATF.

I probably answered 30-40 trace requests in the years I did retail sales in my shop, and the one time I didn't answer a trace request within the mandatory 24 hours (with requested extensions granted without concern) was when I received a trace request by mistake, and after searching all my files again and again, called the wholesaler who had given the erroneous information to the ATF and the trace request was withdrawn. Laguercia had received many more traces than me over the years, and had also responded with the requested information to every, single one.

The fact that the ATF showed up in person and the fact that they called on a Sunday morning and said they wanted to meet Dave the same afternoon told Laguercia that he was sinking into what might possibly be a real mess. His fears were compounded when the same night he gave the 4473 forms to the ATF, President Obama came to Newtown to make his second public statement in three days, and this time he made it clear that the issue of gun violence was squarely within his political radar and that 'something' would get done.[2]

At a memorial service in Newtown on Sunday night, Obama said, "We can't tolerate this any more. These tragedies must end. In the coming weeks, I will use whatever power this office holds to engage my fellow citizens — from law enforcement to mental health professionals to parents and educators — in an effort aimed at preventing more tragedies like this." And every, single gun dealer in America assumed, as it turned out correctly, that this 'effort' would include some attempt to more strictly regulate guns.

Interestingly, although the Sandy Hook rampage was the fourth mass shooting that took place since Obama was inaugurated for his first term in January 2009, the President had been reluctant to push the gun issue as a legislative priority, even when, on January 8, 2011, a member of Congress, Rep. Gabby Giffords, was gunned down in the parking lot of a shopping mall while she was holding a 'meet and greet' for constituents in the middle of the day.[3]

Obama's fear of getting out front on the gun issue was no doubt partially the result of the reaction to his 'clinging to guns and religion' comment during the 2008 primary campaign, a verbal slip which the pro-gun movement always used as 'proof' that the President was not friendly towards gun owners or their guns. But the public reaction to Sandy Hook was so intense that Obama would be swept up in the wave of emotion that began to crest within a day or two of the shooting and push him to move gun-control legislation to a head. Meanwhile, from Friday afternoon until the following Wednesday, Laguercia kept Riverview Sales closed because he was already starting to be a target of the immense public anger which surged throughout the country, aided and abetted by a virtual media invasion into the Newtown which would continue for weeks and months on end.

Riverview Sales re-opened for business on Thursday, December 20. By this time, Laguercia knew that he was somewhere within the vortex of events and attention which erupted following the attack, if only because various public officials, such as Connecticut's Governor, Danell Malloy, were also speaking up about the need to look at legislative responses to mass shootings, and Laguercia knew that this didn't mean that life would be made easier for anyone selling guns. He also knew, thanks to endless media announcements, that the Attorney General, Eric Holder, was coming up to Newtown to meet with Malloy and other interested parties, and Holder just happened to be the boss of the ATF. And it couldn't just be a coincidence that the ATF had physically come to his gun shop in order to get their hands on the paperwork which positively verified his location had supplied Nancy Lanza with her guns

The real reason why the ATF met Laguercia at Riverside Sales started to become apparent when Dave received a text message the following Thursday afternoon. Earlier that day, he and Randi had left Riverview, stopped off for lunch and then made a trip to his bank. When they left the shop, they noticed that a video production van from the CBS affiliate, WFSB - Channel 3 in Hartford, was parked across the street. The same van had been near the store after the news first went around about Nancy Lanza's purchase of guns, but it was interesting that the van had now returned even though general media interest in Laguercia's operation had already started to die down.

The IM, which Dave received shortly after he and Randi came back from the bank, was from a reporter who had been covering the meeting between Malloy, Holder and other officials that took place at the main Fire Station in Newtown early Thursday afternoon. The IM asked whether Dave was aware that the ATF was planning to show up at his shop, a visit that had originally been planned for 3 p.m. but was now apparently common knowledge amongst the media people who were swarming around Newtown and Sandy Hook.

So at least Laguercia now knew why the Channel 3 news truck was parked outside the store, and this van would shortly be joined by other media vehicles when the ATF, in full battle gear, rolled up to the shop in two Humvees sometime between 5 and 6 P.M. The ATF raiding party consisted of 21 or 22 men and women wearing tactical gear, camo uniforms, some of them armed. They trooped in followed by several ATF agents whom Dave recognized as being the same group that had conducted an inspection of the shop the previous year. And then following the squad of what Wayne LaPierre once called 'jack-booted storm troopers,'[4] were representatives of the print and digital media, all of whom had obviously been alerted by the ATF to come along for the ride and cover the event.

The first thing several of the armed and battle-ready agents did was walk up to Laguercia, hand him a search warrant and ask if he was carrying a gun.[5] Two SWAT wannabes then grabbed Randi and began pawing through her purse looking for a gun, as well as patting down the jacket she was wearing to make sure she wasn't going to pull out a weapon and start blazing away. As of this moment, Laguercia and his wife were no longer just the owners of a retail store, they were evidently presumed to be a possible threat to the safety of the ATF team that had just come in through the front door. In the midst of this confusion Dave noticed that one of the agents was talking to another one and pointing at the back door, and it was at that point he realized that the meeting between himself and an ATF agent (who was one of the non-military personnel now standing in the shop) had been not just for the purpose of picking up some paperwork but also giving the ATF an opportunity to get the lay of the land, so to speak, and station additional members of the invasion force out back.

The ATF also handed Dave what they stated was an 'emergency revocation' of his FFL, meaning that as of the moment of their entrance into Riverview, the store could no longer sell any guns. The revocation order was dated the same day as the raid, it was based on meetings between Dave and the ATF in Boston on August 8-9, 2012, these meetings having been concluded with the ATF telling Dave that he could expect a 90-day, temporary license suspension to clear up paperwork management issues found in the inspection carried out the previous year.

Despite the great danger and threat posed by an unarmed, 56-year old retailer and his equally unarmed wife, the ATF successfully secured the gun shop and then began to get to work. And what the work consisted of was going from display cabinet to display cabinet, counting every gun in the store and comparing the final in-store inventory to the black spaces in Dave's A&D. This process took several hours, and at one point Dave noticed the head of the faux-military unit engrossed in a very detailed and somewhat intense discussion with the ATF agent who led the compliance group and was also the agent who had met Dave at the shop on Sunday to pick up the 4473 forms belonging to Nancy Lanza.

This conversation between the two ATF squad leaders was so serious that Dave began to suspect that perhaps they had really found something in the store which might cause him serious problems, up to and including the possibility of his arrest. He quietly moved himself close enough to this conference to overhear what was being said, and it turned out that what was being discussed in total seriousness were the number and type of pizza pies that were going to be ordered and as the field rations for the invading force. After all, it wasn't every day that an ATF battle group had to figure out how many slices each male and female warrior might eat; ordering pies was one thing but making sure that the pies sported the correct combinations of sausage, onions, pepperoni, egg plant and other toppings wasn't a job for just any ordinary man. A task of this sort required planning and teamwork, all of which had to be executed flawlessly in the middle of a battle zone.

If I'm sounding a bit sarcastic, it's by design. Because the 4473 forms, copies of which Laguercia had given the ATF the previous Sunday, couldn't have been more correct. And if his behavior in any way constituted a risk to public safety, nobody in the raiding party had bothered to inform him about the grave threat that either he or Randi represented to the community at large. In fact, when the ATF commandos first charged into the shop, one of them waved a piece of paper in front of Laguercia, informing him that the ATF had decided to declare an 'emergency revocation' of his federal firearms license, and that was that. He was never informed as to any specific reason why he couldn't continue selling guns, nor does the ATF even have any kind of published regulation which describes what an 'emergency revocation' of an FFL actually entails.[6] All that Laguercia knew was that when the ATF raiding party finally finished scoffing down their pizza slices and made to withdraw from the battlefield, he was told that he could no longer display any guns to the public and his federal paperwork – A&D register and 4473 forms – was being taken down to Hartford for a complete and thorough search.

As the ATF packed up their gear, then made ready to depart and piled into their battle wagons with the media beginning to disperse as well, the good news was that neither Dave nor Randi had been arrested, not that the ATF had found or would ever find anything that could conceivably require Mr. or Mrs. Laguercia to be detained. On the other hand, the entire episode was so bizarre that, as Dave told me when I first spoke to him about this event, nothing would have surprised him that evening, up to and including getting thrown in jail.

But to the extent that the activities which transpired in Riverview Sales on Thursday, December 20, could be thought of as a series of inexplicable events in some kind of ongoing drama tied to the emotional tidal wave unleased by Sandy Hook, what then happened was even more inexplicable given the basis upon which new developments piled up one on top of the other. To begin, despite repeated calls by Laguercia's attorney to the ATF, the agency refused either to discuss the matter while, as they claimed, the inspection of his paperwork was still an 'open case.' But even more absurd were the stories which began to come out in the media – stories that could only have been planted by the ATF even while the so-called 'open' investigation was still taking place.

On December 21, the day after the ATF closed down the Riverview shop, a regional newspaper, the Register Citizen News, carried a lead story complete with an exterior photograph of Riverview which was headlined, *'Store that sold guns used in Newtown shooting has troubled history,'*[7] and started off by mentioning that the shop "came under scrutiny by the U.S. Bureau of Alcohol, Tobacco, Firearms and Explosives five years ago, when owner David LaGuercia told investigators that 33 guns were missing from his store."

Now doesn't this sound like the ATF busted a major theft at the shop? In fact, it was Dave who caught the thief, a part-time employee who started lifting guns out of the store inventory during the time that Dave was moving from his initial location in Enfield, CT, down to East Windsor. The employee-turned-thief, who later pleaded guilty to a charge based on videos which Dave gave the ATF to back up his accusations, thought he could spirit away some guns because such a large pile was being transferred from one location to another.

The same article then went on to say that Riverview Sales "was also where Omar Thornton bought the pair of handguns he used to kill eight people and himself inside a Hartford beer distributor in August 2010." A similar story appeared the next day in The New York Post, one of many New York media outlets that sent representatives to Newtown following the shooting.[8] In fact the gun Thornton used for his rampage were not purchased at Riverview, but at Hoffman's Gun Shop in Newington, CT, a fact that was mentioned in the Post article even though their report still asserted that Thornton bought the guns he used in the Hartford Budweiser Distributorship from Riverview.

In addition to the false reporting about Thornton, the profile of Laguercia as a rogue dealer was enhanced and enlarged by stories about another series of gun thefts at Riverview committed the previous year by a 26-year old named Jordan Marsh, who walked out of the store with 11 or 12 rifles over a period of two months. Marsh was able to commit these thefts because the store had recently been required to install a second exit in the front, and the only place this could be accomplished was alongside a series of display cases which made it difficult for sales staff to watch anyone leaving through the secondary door. This area of the store also contained several open displays of used, rifles, most of which were old, surplus guns, as opposed to the new rifles which were only displayed on wall racks kept out of customer reach.

The rifles that Marsh surreptitiously snuck out to his car came from the inventory of used guns sitting on the floor, and when a shop staffer finally saw Marsh taking away one of these rifles, he copied down the plate number, police were contacted and went to Marsh's home where all the stolen guns were found. Marsh would be convicted and given a suspended sentence, Laguercia had the guns returned and the ATF, who had been contacted by local police not only were unconcerned about the fact that a number of guns had been stolen, but told Laguercia that he was the 'victim' in this event and they were pleased that he had been able to prevent the situation from going any further. No mention was made by anyone connected to this investigation that Laguercia had been either inattentive or indifferent to any of the security issues involved in the theft of these guns.

The day before the rampage at Sandy Hook, Jordan Marsh returned to Riverview, walked up to the counter where new long guns were displayed, grabbed a 50-caliber Barrett sniper rifle and ran out the front door. He was briefly chased into the parking lot by store employees but managed to drive off in his car. The police were immediately called, the next day he was arrested, the gun returned to Riverview, and for the second time Marsh was found guilty of stealing guns in early 2014. When the cops arrested Marsh for the theft of the 50-caliber rifle, they also found in his possession an AR-15 that had evidently been taken out of the store the previous week, a theft which wasn't noticed at the time by either Laguercia or anyone else. Now let's go back to the media story about Riverview's 'troubled history.'

The ATF raid on Thursday, December 20, was described by authorities as 'not related' to Sandy Hook, even though virtually every media story about what the ATF referred to as 'enforcement activity' connected this incident to the sale of guns to Nancy Lanza, transfers which the media initially learned through comments made to them by the ATF. One of the media stories that surfaced after the raid mentioned that the ATF agents who entered the store on Thursday night couldn't locate some 50 guns which, according to the A&D register, were supposed to still be inside the store. In fact, the reason these guns went unnoticed in the search conducted by the ATF was because they were sitting in a display case, the top of which was covered by the pizzas that the raiding party had brought in to serve as their field rations during their maneuvers within the store.

The week following the raid, Laguercia was informed by the Federal attorney in Hartford, Robert Spector, that the Government was going to indict him for a felony within the next 30 days unless he was willing to enter into immediate negotiations to plead to a lesser charge. Dave's attorney immediately asked the Government to postpone any action because such a deal might have caused his client to lose a substantial sum of money, upwards of $500,000, the value of the guns which he still owned but would be unable to sell and possibly entirely lose if the guns were forfeited to the ATF. Spector's office turned down this request and Laguercia ended up selling the entire inventory to a gun store in Maine, the fire sale resulting in a significant financial loss.

Notwithstanding Spector's bluster, Laguercia's attorney was able to hem and haw the government for nearly eight months, with Dave eventually pleading to two misdemeanor charges in August, 2013. I'm going to talk about the sentencing and its aftermath in Chapter 5, but right now I want to return to the manner and the timing in of the government's assault on Dave. And I will go into details about this issue by first quoting a statement about Laguercia which appeared in a report, 'Lost and Stolen Guns from Gun Dealers,' published by The Center for American Progress in 2013.[9] The Center, known as CAP, is considered the premier liberal think-tank in Washington, D.C., and much of its research and publications helps create the narrative which then ends up defining Democratic Party policy initiatives both within legislation and political campaigns.

This particular article begins with the following statement: "Every year tens of thousands of guns are discovered to be missing from the inventories of federally licensed gun dealers. Guns that go missing from dealer inventories, whether they are stolen, illegally sold without proper documentation, or misplaced due to negligent recordkeeping, pose two main risks to public safety: (1). Guns stolen from dealers often end up in criminal hands. (2). Guns lost or stolen from dealers are more difficult to trace because there is no record of who initially purchased the gun from the dealer."

The article then went on to list 16 gun dealers as 'high-profile examples' of dealers whose business practices resulted in scores of missing guns, including a description of Riverview Sales, which stated that: "The day after the Sandy Hook shooting, a man was arrested at Riverview for stealing a .50 caliber firearm, and further investigation revealed that he had stolen a second gun from the store four days earlier and nine additional guns from the store in 2011. The store's owner said he was unaware of these thefts and was described by a local detective as 'nonchalant' and 'a very non-caring gun owner, very lax in his paperwork.' For these violations, ATF initiated a revocation action against Riverview on December 20, 2013."

This entire section of the CAP report on Riverview began, of course, with a statement that this was the store which sold Nancy Lanza her guns. Now here are the true facts contrary to what the CAP report said. First, the 'man' arrested for stealing the Barrett 50-caliber gun was Jordan Marsh, who was not arrested at the shop even though it was a call made by the shop to the police that resulted in Marsh's later arrest. Second, the guns that were stolen in 2011 surfaced because someone saw Marsh running out of the store with a gun. Third and most important, the ATF's revocation action against Riverview was initiated and finalized in 2012, December 20, 2012, to be exact.

The revocation order was personally handed to Laguercia when the ATF riot squad charged into his shop on December 20, 2012. It followed a meeting at the ATF Boston office between Laguercia and ATF officials on August 8-9, 2012 for the purposes of reviewing a report based on an inspection of his records initiated in January 2011 by the IOI squad of the ATF.[10] Note, incidentally, that the Boston meeting occurred more than 18 months after the inspection commenced at Dave's shop, during which time he probably sold 7,000 or 8,000 guns. The fact that the ATF considered him to be such a risk to public safety on December 20, 2012, while at the same time allowing him to continue selling an enormous quantity of guns to the public, makes it somewhat difficult to accept the government's argument that all of a sudden he represented a serious threat to public safety, given the fact that the violations for which he was cited in the 2012 revocation were essentially the same as violations found in inspections conducted in 2007 and 2009.

Following the 2007 inspection, Dave was cited for inaccuracy in 4473 forms, mistakes in the A&D book, missing multiple-sale forms and missing information on NICS background checks. Following the 2009 inspection, he was cited for exactly the same mistakes. I was also cited for the same mistakes after the ATF inspected my store. Now in fact, because he acknowledged the mistakes that were found in the 2007 inspection, the existence of such errors identified again in 2009 meant that Dave was guilty of 'willful' violations of procedures, for which his federal firearms license could have been revoked at that time. The only thing that happened after the 2009 inspection was the same thing that happened after 2007, namely, Dave had to sit through a meeting with ATF staff to review all his mistakes, sign a letter pledging to be a good boy, and back to the shop.

Here are the relevant quotes from the 2012 Revocation order itself:

On February 13, 2008, the licensee [Laguercia] attending [sic] a warning conference at ATF's Hartford, Connecticut office. At the conference the violations discovered during the 2007 inspection, as well as how to correct them and avoid future violations, were discussed. ATF sent (and the licensee received) a letter summarizing the discussions that had taken place at the warning conference, warning the licensee that he should expect future inspections, and reminding the licensee that future violations may be considered willful and may result in the revocation of the federal firearms license.

Now here is the text of the letter that Laguercia received following his 2009 inspection:

On January 7, 2010, the licensee attended a warning conference at ATF's Hartford, Connecticut office. At the conference the violations discovered during the 2007 inspection, as well as how to correct them and avoid future violations, were discussed. ATF sent (and the licensee received) a letter summarizing the discussions that had taken place at the warning conference, warning the licensee that he should expect future inspections, and reminding the licensee that future violations may be considered willful and may result in the revocation of the federal firearms license.

The only difference in the content of those letters was the date. Otherwise, what the ATF told Laguercia about willful violations in 2008, was repeated word for word in 2010 following the inspection which occurred in 2009. Yet in neither instance did the ATF find it necessary to do anything except remind Laguercia that errors had been found in both inspections which were willfully committed and could have resulted in a revocation of his federal firearms license except that the ATF declined to act. And it should be noted, incidentally, that while the ATF went to great lengths to identify the various violations in both inspections, at no time did they state how they arrived at a decision to let Laguercia off the hook.

Now we come to the report for the 2011 inspection which, like the two previous inspections, found various paperwork and procedural errors in both the A&D register and the 4473 forms. Although the 2011 report was much more detailed regarding the specific paperwork mistakes found in both the A&D and 4473 documentation, the bottom line is that once again all this report basically showed was that

Laguercia and various employees were frequently overwhelmed by the volume of paperwork on days when they sold lots of guns, and nobody bothered to go back and check every, single entry on every, single form to make sure that no mistakes might later be found.

The previous paragraph may sound like something of an excuse to explain away the sloppiness of Laguercia and his staff. But the fact is that none of the errors committed by people selling guns at Riverview could be taken to support the idea that some kind of rogue behavior was going on. If mistakes made on gun-related forms were so serious and could have contributed to guns ending up in the wrong hands, how come in all the years that Dave operated he was never accused of being unable to answer a trace, never accused of being the subject of a large number of ATF traces of crime guns, never accused as being the source for guns that were picked up in the street?

The only times that guns left the store in unauthorized fashion was when they were stolen and these activities, once realized, were immediately reported to the police. Further, the fact that a gun is missing because it has been swiped out the door isn't, in and of itself, a violation by a federal firearms licensee of any law at all. The law requires the licensee to report a stolen or missing gun and he can be sanctioned if the report is not made in timely fashion; i.e., 48 hours from when the gun is found to be missing or lost. But the law does not require a dealer to have any kind of system which would allow him to be alerted the moment a gun walked out of the shop. The 2011 inspection report on Riverview did not and could not mention the guns which were stolen from the shop by Jordan Marsh in 2011, yet the ATF's rush into Riverview Sales on December 20 was allegedly because Marsh had walked out with several more guns.

Finally, the 2011 inspection report contained a curious reference to the sale of guns on two separate occasions to a Massachusetts resident whom it was claimed did not possess a state-issued license from Massachusetts enabling him to purchase or own guns. This is the only instance in the entire litany of charges against Laguercia which could be viewed as giving someone a gun who didn't qualify to own a gun; in other words, a straw sale or gun trafficking as it is sometimes called. Are there gun dealers who sell guns this way and should be stopped? Yes. Was Dave Laguercia one of those dealers? No. And here's the reason why.

Connecticut, like many states, operates under what is called a 'contiguous state' rule. What this means is that if you come into Connecticut from an adjacent state like Massachusetts, and purchase a long gun (but not a handgun), fill out a 4473 form and pass the background check, you can then take the gun back to your state of residence and stick it in your home. If Connecticut did not have such a rule (which they no longer have as a result of a change in the state gun law in 2014) the background check would not have been approved because the FBI examiner would have realized that the purchase was being made by a non-resident and therefore would not go through. But this particular individual, who came into Riverview twice and each time purchased a surplus rifle, entered the correct information on the 4473 form, the NICS response was a 'proceed,' and Dave was under no obligation to ask the customer whether he could legally own the gun in his home state.

I live in Massachusetts and from time to time drive up I-91 to Vermont to shop in Brattleboro, which happens to have a great outdoor store – Sam's – which used to carry a wonderful inventory of Marlin lever-action rifles and I'm a sucker for lever-action guns from way back. How many times did I walk into Sam's and buy a Marlin off the rack, fill out the 4473 and then take the gun back to Massachusetts and stick it with all the other 'must have' guns which are probably still sitting exactly where I plopped them when I brought them home? About as many times as my wife walked into the shoe store up the block from Sam's and bought herself a new pair of shoes which, in her case, probably were worn more times than those Marlins were ever taken out by me and shot.

But never let anyone try and convince you that gun nuts buy guns in order to shoot them. We buy guns because we like guns, and there's no law which says that as a Massachusetts resident I can't still go to Vermont, New Hampshire, Maine, New York or Rhode Island and pull out my Visa card, my driver's license and get a gun. I happen to have a gun license issued by the Bay State but I have never been asked to show it when I buy a rifle or shotgun in another state.

Looking at Laguercia's business history as dispassionately as possible, one could make the argument that he was certainly a candidate for some degree of disciplinary action by the ATF, if only because as stupid as the paperwork regulations may be, either you abide by them or you don't. And if the cost of running a gun business becomes excessive because you are unable to deal with the required paperwork in a disciplined and effective way, nobody twisted anyone's arm to become a dealer and every gun dealer going in knows that the regulatory environment is both antiquated and ineffective when it comes to preventing violence caused by guns. The fact that the ATF still sends trace requests by fax when the world has gone to email is an indication that the agency is still operating as if things haven't changed since it was given authority to create the regulatory environment and procedures for gun dealers back in 1968.

On the other hand, we can't get away from the fact that if the inspection of Laguercia's operation which began in 1911 revealed him to be such a threat to public safety, how come it took almost a year following the last time that ATF inspectors came into his shop for an audit until a post-inspection meeting was held? And how come following the Boston meeting on August 8-9, it took another 4 months to draft and then deliver a notice of license revocation which happened to occur within a week after the massacre at Sandy Hook?

CHAPTER 5

THE BLAME GAME GETS WORSE

Seven hours after they swarmed into Riverview Sales and with bellies now filled with extra rations of pizza pies, the ATF battle group withdrew from the shop, leaving Dave and Randi to clean up the mess. During the course of the evening Dave had been told that he could no longer sell or receive guns, so to all intents and purposes his career as a gun dealer had just come to an end. At the same time, he was not told that he had 60 days to file an appeal of the revocation, and from the moment he filed the appeal he could continue to sell his gun inventory to retail customers, even though he could not replenish the inventory by receiving additional shipments of guns.

In fact, the notice outlining the appeal procedure was within the 12-page revocation order that he received that evening, but he was about as ready to read the fine print of 12 pages at that moment the way he was ready to take a flying leap off the roof of the shop. Unfortunately, the local attorney who had taken care of various business matters for Dave over the previous years had absolutely no experience at all in anything even remotely connected to guns, or firearms law, or even dealing with a Federal prosecutor's office which was out for blood. In other words, from the moment that the ATF landed on his doorstep, Dave Laguercia was outmanned, and pardon the pun, outgunned.

The degree to which Dave was now falling into a legal quagmire for which his protective resources were basically nil became apparent to him within the next several days, when he went with his lawyer to meet the U.S. Attorney, Robert Spector, who was going to be prosecuting this case. The reason for this meeting at the federal building in Bridgeport, was because Dave had been told at some point Thursday night that in addition to having his federal firearms license revoked, he was also going to be facing a criminal charge.

Under GCA68, any violation of the law is punishable with a jail term of up to five years.[1] And since a mistake on a 4473, such as forgetting to put in the date of the call to NICS, or identifying the gun which was sold as a 9mm instead of a 45 (in my inspection errors like this cropped up again and again), if this is a 'willful' error the licensee has broken the law. This is the reason why the ATF puts so much emphasis on distinguishing between a simple paperwork mistake and a 'willful' mistake, the idea being that if they were to charge someone with a felony for writing 'July 15, 2016,' when it was really 'July 14, 2016,' they would never dare bring something like that into court. But when it is done 'willfully,' i.e., you were told not to do it again and you did it again, in Dave's case he was told multiple times how to fill out the forms, he agreed that he had been told how to do it the proper way, and he still screwed up the paperwork, then obviously he was 'trying' to avoid obeying the law.

Except even here, any decent defense attorney could shoot the government's case full of holes by simply putting his client on the stand and asking him to recount exactly how he was instructed by the ATF to properly fill out the forms. And if the client in question was given the same degree of instruction that I received during and after my inspection, there's every good chance that the felony charge which the dealer was facing for not doing the paperwork correctly would be tossed out. The longest and most detailed conversation I had with the ATF crew who conducted my last inspection – it was the same bunch who were part of the landing party that invaded Dave's store – was a conversation in which I gave the team leader detailed instructions about where to take the team for lunch. Funny how the ATF inspectors always seem most concerned about how and what they are going to eat.

On the rare occasion when a dealer is actually indicted for something having to do with the transfer or sale of guns, the ATF might get some hints about the dealer's illegal behavior from how the books are kept, but invariably the dealer is criminally charged because he is actually directly involved in the unlawful transfer of guns. For example, on June 9, 2017, Jack Fox and Hollie Fox, a man and wife dealer team, were sentenced in Federal Court in Columbus, OH, for selling more than 200 guns without background checks, their particular MO is that after a background check was complete for a legal transfer, they would then add another gun to that 4473 form, then sell the second gun 'off paper' to someone else.[2]

Now that's serious criminality and none of the mistakes which turned up in the Riverview inspections would ever have been considered to be that kind of a crime. Nevertheless, Laguercia was ordered to meet U.S. Attorney Spector in his Bridgeport office where he was informed, in no uncertain terms, that he was going to be facing a felony indictment within 30 days. He was not told what the specific charge or charges would be, but he knew FFL regulations well enough to know that any of the paperwork mistakes which had been glossed over by the ATF in the past might come back to haunt him now.

The first thing Dave did when he got back to the store was to try and figure out what to do with his massive gun inventory, because if he couldn't get rid of all the guns before an indictment dropped on his head, every gun in his possession once the indictment was handed down could become an additional felony charge. And the good news was that while his inventory contained a sizable chunk of 'tactical' guns (military-style AR-15 rifles and so forth) which would experience a brief spurt in demand following Sandy Hook, the bad news was that Dave couldn't afford the time it would take to sell a couple of guns to this dealer here and a couple to that dealer there. So he ended up doing what all storeowners do when they are forced to shut down their store – he loaded the entire pile of guns into his truck, drove 4 hours to Kittery, ME and sold his stock to a big-box store which, of course, gave him a whole lot less than what the guns were actually worth.

Dave continued to keep the store open after dumping the guns, if only because he still had a million dollars or more of non-gun inventory on his shelves which he could continue to sell. But people don't buy ammunition or holsters or other gun accessories in great numbers without being able at least to look at guns. And the only guns that you could now see at Riverview were the pictures of guns in some of the advertising posters that still adorned the walls. Riverview Sales got awfully quiet, awfully fast.

But the public reaction to Sandy Hook hadn't quieted down at all. The day after the ATF's invasion of the Riverview shop, Wayne LaPierre, NRA Executive Vice President, called a press conference to give the 'official,' pro-gun view on Newtown, which was basically a pitch for more guns and more public support for the idea of having armed guards in every school. LaPierre announced a cobbled-together program called The National School Shield program, which he advertised as a combination consulting service, armed-guard training program and advocacy effort all designed to make school environments deal more effectively with the kind of threat represented by what happened at Sandy Hook.[3]

The School Shield program went nowhere, as did the NRA's calls to eliminate gun-free zones. On the other side of the aisle, however, momentum began ramping up for a new attempt to pass a new national gun-control law. Obama first appointed Vice President Joe Biden to head up an effort to draft new policies and then, in mid-January, announced a series of legislative proposals as well as a list of executive actions, the latter not requiring Congressional action and therefore of limited consequence but at least reflecting the direction in which the President intended to go.[4]

In fact, none of the legislative proposals suggested by Obama could have prevented Adam Lanza from grabbing his mother's AR-15 and walking into the elementary school at Sandy Hook, a point which the NRA and its allies repeated again and again every chance they got. But while a new gun law that restricted ownership of assault weapons was quickly voted through the Connecticut Legislature and signed by Governor Malloy in early April 2013, a similar bill re-instating the 1994 assault weapons ban at the national level never had any chance of getting to the President's desk, and a watered-down bill which dropped any reference to assault weapons but did call for background checks on private transfers of guns failed to get out of the Senate by a vote that wasn't even close.[5]

Despite the failure of Congress to act on a gun bill, the continued attention to this issue helped keep the Newtown tragedy front and center in the public eye. Part of this continued public concern with what happened at Sandy Hook on December 20 was fueled by the initial media reaction, as well as the appearance of the President and the political debate that flared up after gun bills were hastily introduced at the federal level, along with new gun-control laws that were quickly passed in Connecticut and New York. But the Newtown event resonated through the public consciousness for one other, important reason, namely, the slaughter of so many young children in a small, well-heeled suburban community that was the quintessential ideal of a place which most Americans would consider to be "safe."

One should not underestimate the degree to which the mass, psychological response to Newtown played a role in shaping and determining the manner in which Dave Laguercia was dealt with by the government, as well as by the digital, television and print press. Once the news got out that the gun used by Adam Lanza had been purchased at Riverview, there were probably as many pictures of the front of the Riverview store as there were pictures of the Sandy Hook school. And despite the fact that at no time did the ATF ever explicitly state that their actions against Dave were in any way connected to Nancy Lanza's purchase of the AR-15, there was never any media coverage of the Riverview situation which did not link him and his store to the massacre at Sandy Hook.

Not only was Laguercia transformed into an individual who somehow bore responsibility for what happened in Newtown, but he faced a public relations onslaught all by himself. On February 26, 2012, a young, African-American man, Trayvon Martin, was gunned down by a self-appointed neighborhood security monitor in Sanford, FL, named George Zimmerman who was subsequently charged with murder but got off. After getting out of bond but before his trial, Zimmerman put up a website to receive donations to help pay his legal costs, receiving almost $200,000 before he took the website down.[6] Between December 20, 2012 and when Laguercia appeared in court to be sentenced on August 24, 2013, Dave received absolutely no calls of support from anyone, nor offers of help of any kind, and calls he and his wife made both to the NRA and the National Shooting Sports Foundation were never returned.

Yet despite the continued attempt of the entire media to connect Laguercia in some way to the murders of 26 people at Sandy Hook, the government's charges against him did not, nor could the charges mention the events at Newtown at all. Which brings us to the question whose answer is the real reason why I wrote this book: Given the fact that the government could and did revoke Laguercia's federal gun license, effectively putting him out of business and ending his business career, why did federal authorities then go the extra mile so to speak, and begin putting together a criminal case? The answer actually begins the day before Adam Lanza shot his way into the elementary school in Sandy Hook.

On Thursday, December 13, 2012, the family of former U.S. Border Patrol Agent Brian Terry filed a lawsuit in Federal court.[7] Terry was a 'former' agent because he was shot and killed two years' previously in a firefight near the U.S.-Mexico border with a gun that was linked to an ATF gun-smuggling investigation – *Fast & Furious* – ostensibly aimed at seizing assault rifles which had been purchased in the U.S., then converted to full-auto weapons and then taken down to Mexico to be used by the drug cartels.

This operation, which was launched under the Bush Administration in 2006 but widened after Obama came into office and named Eric Holder to run the DOJ, was a mess from the beginning, and was finally closed down after Terry's death. As a result of this harebrained scheme the ATF managed to identify a bunch of low-level gun smugglers already known to other law enforcement agencies and force several law-abiding gun dealers to make what they knew were illegal sales. In truth, what motivated the ATF to plan and then carry out this program in Keystone-cops fashion was an effort by the agency to be granted a federal OCEDTF (Organized Crime Drug Enforcement Task Force) wiretap which had never previously been approved for ATF use, but would, if approved for this operation, enhance the ATF's standing in law enforcement circles, tantamount to being recognized as equal to the FBI and the DEA.[8]

The ATF got their wiretap, ramped up the program after Holder became their new boss, but other than Brian Terry getting killed, they basically got nothing accomplished at all. Within a month after Terry's death, all hell broke loose in Washington as Republicans, beginning to think about the 2012 election cycle realized they had the possibility of a ready-made political scandal on their hands. By mid-2011 there were at least four investigations going forward, including one led by Republican Charles Grassley in the Senate and another by Republican Darrell Issa in the House. Obama didn't help himself in March when he publicly disavowed any responsibility for an investigation conducted by an agency under his own Justice Department's control; Holder made the entire situation more problematic when he later stated that he didn't know anything about *Fast & Furious* even though it then turned out that he might have been briefed on the situation a year before.[9]

If Republicans like Grassley and Issa hadn't been so obsessed with using their hearings to score political points against a man who would soon be running again for President, they might have actually conducted a serious and probing study as to how the government's agency responsible for regulating the firearm business could have consciously allowed several thousand guns to be purchased in the United States, smuggled into Mexico and then lost sight of to the point that the ATF ultimately had to admit that they didn't even know how many guns were 'walked out' of the country in this way.

On June 28, 2012, following his seventh appearance before a Congressional committee investigating Fast & Furious, Eric Holder became the first member of a sitting Cabinet to be charged with criminal contempt by Congress, a vote that was taken along party lines in the House of Representatives, by which time the 2012 Presidential election was in full swing.[10] In September, a report from the DOJ's Inspector General basically cleared Holder of any wrongdoing but indicated serious management problems within the ATF.[11] The November election results, of course, shielded both Obama and Holder from any further political repercussions from the Fast

& Furious mess, but then Terry's family submitted a law suit which elevated public awareness about ATF shortcomings again.

What I am suggesting is that the decision to go beyond Laguercia's license revocation and tack on a criminal charge was not based on any kind of criminal behavior at all. And to the extent that what he did could be considered criminal 'acts' in the most narrow sense of the word, the timing of the raid on the gun shop which sold the Sandy Hook gun should not be dismissed simply as a coincidence, but must be understood within the context of events which made Dave Laguercia a perfect target for the actions of a law enforcement agency whose reputation certainly needed to be protected if not improved.

To understand the full dimensions of the problem facing the ATF, we need to go back and briefly examine the revocation order again. In addition to the endless list of paperwork errors, which the ATF had not considered important enough to sanction Laguercia in any way following inspections in 2007 and 2009, this report also included two instances in which a Riverview employee, Krys Dibella violated ATF rules by selling ammunition to a known felon, Wilfred Hellebrand, whose girlfriend had purchased guns and ammunition in the shop. While Dibella was the individual who committed the violations (for which he would be charged and given probation at a later date) because he held the federal gun license, Laguercia could also be charged.

These issues were discussed by the ATF and Laguercia at the two-day meeting in Boston on August 8-9, 2012. The charges against Dibella were again mentioned in the media stories following Laguercia's March 24, 2014 court appearance when he pled guilty to two misdemeanors, and were repeated again when Laguercia returned to court to be sentenced on August 2014. But the behavior of Dibella, which was used by the government to picture Dave Laguercdia as a rogue dealer running an out-of-control retail operation, needs to be not only explained in terms of what actually happened, but more important, placed into a proper chronological perspective in order to better understand what the case that was built against Laguercia was really all about.

For that information we have to turn to the pre-sentencing memorandum which Laguercia's attorney, Robert Altchiler, filed on his behalf, before the sentencing in federal court took place.[12] It should also be noted that the federal magistrate, Holly Fitzsimmons, also received pre-sentencing reports from the Federal Department of Probation that recommended only a 'short period of probation and a financial penalty [which is] adequate to address the conduct in the offense of conviction.' Altchiler's memorandum went on to say that no evidence had been produced which showed that "Mr. LaGuercia has never knowingly permitted a firearm to be sold to a prohibited person and has never failed to effectively assist any request for a trace of a weapon. Importantly, the paperwork failures have never impacted the government's ability to quickly trace any weapon sold at Riverview." The federal prosecutor did not contest any of these statements.

As to the Dibella situation, here again Laguercia did not argue against the fact that without his knowledge, an employee violated the law which made Laguercia legally responsible for what the employee did. Indeed, during the Boston meeting, the ATF acknowledged that Laguercia had not been aware of Dibella's illegal behavior until the agency brought it to Dave's attention on July 7, 2012, almost a year after Dibella's illegal behavior was first brought to the attention of the ATF when the felon, Wilfred Hellebrand, was arrested in a drug sting. This arrest occurred around the same time that the ATF was wrapping up its 2011 inspection of Riverview, and Hellebrand's connection to Riverview was discovered during a search of his car when a Riverview store invoice for ammunition turned up.

What this means is that the ATF knew about Dibella's illegal behavior but withheld telling Laguercia about his rogue employee for more than a year. And when the ATF finally got around to informing Laguercia about Dibella, Dave immediately fired the employee who later was then charged with selling ammunition to a 'known' felon, along with allowing this felon access to guns. But in fact the ATF admitted that the evidence of Dibella's illegality; i.e., selling ammunition to someone whom he knew could not buy or possess the product, didn't come from Dibella, it came from Hellebrand and his girlfriend, the latter claiming that *she* told Dibella that her boyfriend was a felon, notwithstanding the fact that Hellebrand was never actually charged for possession of ammunition, which is as much of a federal offense as selling the ammo to someone you know is prohibited from possessing ammo or guns.

Now here's the most interesting part of this little episode. In fact, when Dave met the ATF at his shop on Sunday, December 16, 2012 and willingly gave them the 4473 forms filled out by Nancy Lanza when she purchased her two guns, the ATF realized that it was none other than Krys Dibella who filled out the paperwork that went with both sales. And lo and behold, it turned out that there was a clerical mistake on the 4473 covering the purchase of the AR-15, because the date on which the NICS check was conducted and the date of the sale were different by one day. But as Laguercia's attorney pointed out to the Court, in the period between when the ATF learned about Dibella's alleged misconduct and when Laguercia was informed about same, his employee personally sold more than 3,000 guns and yet the ATF did not consider his behavior to be any kind of risk until they spotted the 4473 filled out by Nany Lanza which also contained Dibella's name.

Why am I asking the reader to wade through so much petty detail about the behavior of one Riverview employee who may or may not have illegally sold ammunition to a guy who wasn't supposed to be able to buy such an item in the first place? Because there was never a story about Laguercia in the media which didn't mention Dibella to show that there were other serious issues involving problems far beyond sloppy paperwork and inattention to clerical details. Virtually every one of those stories was based on statements or leaks made by government and/or law enforcement personnel because Dave Laguercia, who is not known to be verbally reticent (remember, he was a successful used car dealer before getting into guns) kept his mouth shut for the entire period between December 20, 2012, up to and including today.

On the other hand, no such restraint was exhibited by law enforcement authorities when it came to comments about Laguercia and his shop designed to paint him in the most unflattering terms. A newspaper story the day after the shop was closed down stated that Riverview was raided for "reasons not related to the December 14th shooting at Sandy Hook." Yet when asked why the raid took place, an East Windsor police detective was quoted as ominously saying, "there are so many other reasons."[13] So while the government took pains to describe and justify the ATF action against Dave as somehow completely unconnected to the events which occurred in Newtown the previous week, the government was also trying to build a case against Laguercia that would justify not only punitive, bureaucratic sanctions, but criminal sanctions as well.

I have searched as far as possible into ATF public documents and cannot find a single instance in which a federally-licensed dealer had his license revoked and then faced criminal charges, unless it was his criminal behavior which brought him to the attention of law enforcement and an inspection of his records then provided evidence which allowed a criminal prosecution to commence. This is exactly the reverse of what happened in Laguercia's case, where the ATF could not connect any of the paperwork sloppiness to a single, criminal act of any kind. Hence, the necessity to connect the dots between Laguercia and Dibella, even as the ATF acknowledged that Laguercia was completely in the dark about Dibella's behavior which was used to create the image of Laguercia as a danger to public safety.

Going back to the Boston meeting on August 8-9 2012, discussions took place between Laguercia and the ATF about what type of penalty would be appropriate to meet the agency's concerns regarding the continued lack of controls over paperwork, while at the same time recognizing that, in and of itself, none of Laguercia's mistakes represented anything more than a lack of attention or training or perhaps both. The final conference on this issue, which obviously took place prior to December 14, was that Laguercia would accept a temporary revocation of his license for a period of perhaps three months, using this time to develop a better paperwork management system as well as a proper educational program for staff.

Since there was not a single issue mentioned in the Revocation Order served on December 20 that had not been discussed at the Boston meeting four months' previously, how can one explain the dramatic change in ATF tone and attitude when the commando unit arrived on December 20, complete with guns, tactical outfits, and along with the Revocation Order also slapped Laguercia with a federal search & seizure warrant as the troops invaded the store? Let's not forget that it was Laguercia who took it upon himself to notify the ATF on Friday, December 14, that he had not only sold a Sig P226 pistol to Nancy Lanza, the transaction which was the subject of the ATF trace, but that he had also sold her the AR-15 which, at that time, the ATF knew nothing about at all. He then voluntarily agreed to drop what he was doing and meet the ATF agents at his shop on Sunday to give them, at their request, the original 4473 forms for both transactions, even though ATF rules stipulate that original documentation remains in the location where it was created and all trace documentation is copied and sent to ATF by fax.

The fact that the ATF marched into Riverview with a search warrant could only mean that what had been an inspection of paperwork conducted in his shop was now being turned into a full-fledged criminal investigation, even though at no time was Laguercia ever told that anything he had ever done could be considered a criminal offense, unless one uses the word 'criminal' to characterize sloppy paperwork and incomplete or erroneous forms. In fact, what was clearly happening at Riverview Sales beginning on December 20, 2012 and going all the way through Laguercia's final court appearance for sentencing on March 27, 2014,[14] was an attempt by law enforcement authorities, particularly the ATF, to create a self-fulfilling portrait of a man who was a danger to society because in some way or another, he had played some role and was responsible in some way for what happened at Sandy Hook.

The attempt to create a causal linkage between Laguercia and the Sandy Hook rampage was so evident that it was mentioned in, among all places, the pre-sentence report issued by the Federal Department of Probation and filed with Magistrate Holly Fitzsimmons before Laguercia appeared for sentencing in her Court. Here is a word-for-word excerpt from the Probation report: "Mr. LaGuercia is the one who has to answer for one of his employees selling a firearm to a prohibited person and another incident where a firearm was stolen out of his store, in plain view of other employees and customers. In regard to the blame, shaming and media attention Mr. LaGuercia and Riverview Sales, Inc has received as a result of the shooting on December 14, 2012, the words and reports seem unjust."

What the government's own pre-sentencing memorandum is saying was that the comments being made about Laguercia were not some random, offhand statements which get bandied back and forth between media people and the folks with whom they speak just because everyone needs some extra content to keep pace with the non-stop information cycle that now characterizes internet news. Rather, the Department of Probation's statement was a recognition that a directed, organized and concerted campaign to blame Laguercia for Sandy Hook began to emerge from the moment on December 20 that Dave received an IM telling him that the ATF was going to raid his shop.

The source of that IM was a reporter from Hartford's CBS affiliate who had just seen a tweet from another reporter, Len Besthoff, who worked for the NBC Hartford affiliate and was eager to announce that the ATF raid of Riverview was going to take place later that afternoon. And how did Besthoff get the scoop on the planned raid? He had been hanging around the main fire station at Newtown where a meeting involving various government officials was taking place. This confab, which took place after a morning meeting at the White House involving four Cabinet officials: Janet Napolitano of Homeland Security, Arne Duncan who ran the Department of Education, Kathleen Sebelius of HHS and Eric Holder, chief lawman of the United States, met with Joe Biden who was now in charge of a taskforce to plan what was called a 'meaningful response' to the Sandy Hook event. Following this meeting, Attorney General Holder flew up to Newtown for a meeting at the firehouse which was closed to the public but ran until after 5 P.M.[14]

At 2:39 P.M., while the closed-door meeting involving Holder, Malloy and ATF officials was going on in the Newtown Fire Department headquarters, Besthoff sent out this tweet: **"Apparent ATF raid @ store where Lanza bought gun OnlyOn3 #wfsb."**[15] Recall that Dave and Randi Laguercia had noticed a Channel 3 media van parked outside their shop when they left Riverview around noon that day to eat lunch and go to the bank.

At 3:51 P.M. came a second Besthoff tweet: **"Sources: Riverview Gun Sales in East Windsor CT sold #NancyLanza at least one of guns used in #Newtown #wfsb."** Recall that the only person with whom Laguercia had shared this information was the ATF agent who contacted him the previous Friday afternoon regarding the Sig P226, and it was Laguercia who first alerted the ATF to the sale of the AR-15.

At 4:49 P.M. came the next tweet: **"#RiverviewGunSales got on radar screen after man with mental issues tried stealing 50 caliber long gun Saturday #wfsb."** Recall it was a store employee who ran after the 'man with mental issues,' wrote his license number and then told Laguercia to contact the police.

Then at 4:52 P.M: **"Upon further investigation, police learned same man with mental issues succesfully stole AR-15 from #RiverviewGunSales 4 days earlier #wfsb"** The 'further investigation' was the fact that the cops tracked Jordan Marsh to a motel room at Bradley Airport and found him in possession of the AR-15 which no store employee saw him stealing from Riverview but, in fact, the police had been looking for him after the previous theft was reported to them by Dave.

The last tweet at 4:53 P.M: **"police say this same man with mental issues stole 11 other weapons from #RiverviewGunSales, found in June 2011 @ father's home #wfsb."** When these guns were returned to Riverview, the ATF and local law enforcement told Laguercia that he was "the victim" of these thefts, not the instigator nor in any way to be blamed for the behavior of Jordan Marsh.

All of these tweets from Len Besthoff, repeated in media stories published both locally and nationally, were pushed out while the meeting in Newtown attended by Holder and the other government officials was still going on. Nevertheless, Besthoff could have only been given this information from someone who was attending that meeting or someone who had access to the facts about Jordan Marsh and the purchase by Nancy Lanza of the two guns. The Jordan Marsh information could have been shared with Besthoff by local law enforcement authorities, the information about the source of the AR-15 that was used to mow down the students and teachers at Sandy Hook could only have come from the ATF.

Am I saying or implying that Eric Holder participated in discussions, the purposes of which were to connect Dave Laguercia's behavior as the owner of the gun shop where Nancy Lanza bought the AR-15 to the murder rampage then committed by her son? I am and I am not. I made three separate attempts to contact Eric Holder at his Covington & Burling office, I made it clear that I wrote a weekly column on gun violence for Huffington Post and was writing a book on Sandy Hook and neither he nor anyone connected to him at the law firm bothered to respond to my calls. Holder's refusal to engage me in a brief conversation about Sandy Hook should not be taken as an indication as to whether or not he was in any way connected to the conscious leaking of information from the ATF to the media regarding the behavior of Dave Laguercia or the history of Riverview Sales. But only the ATF and Laguercia knew where Nancy Lanza purchased the AR-15 prior to this information becoming public knowledge on December 20, so the decision to push this information into the public domain had to come from somewhere within the ATF chain of command.

Once the media began talking about the ATF raid of Riverview, and particularly since not a single media story correctly disclosed the degree to which Laguercia had been cooperating fully with ATF and other law enforcement authorities prior to the raid, the profile of Laguercia as being in some way responsible for what happened at Sandy Hook became the narrative which continued to inform and shape the news. And this narrative remained the government's core argument against Laguercia up to his sentencing appearance as well, with the Department of Justice charging that Dave had conducted his business in a "lax and irresponsible way." The fact that the ATF did not take any action against Dave for his 'irresponsible' behavior over a period of five years since his behavior came to their attention, the fact that they withheld from him knowledge of an employee's illegal behavior for more than a year, the fact that he was never accused of having done anything other than a sloppy bookkeeping job, these issues were never mentioned by the government in their headlong rush to show that something had been 'done' in response to what happened at Sandy Hook.

In fact, no matter what Obama promised when he came to Newtown the Sunday after the shooting, the only thing the government specifically did in response to Sandy Hook was to create a post-event storyline which made them appear to be taking decisive action against the gun dealer who sold Nancy Lanza the AR-15. And since the sale was conducted in entirely legal fashion, and since the shooter who then used the gun couldn't be charged with anything because he was dead, Dave Laguercia was next in line.

If I seem overly paranoid about wanting to create a conspiracy to peddle misleading information somewhere within the ATF chain of command, bear in mind the fact that the ATF has a long and hallowed tradition for promoting stories about their law-enforcement prowess which simply do not align with the truth. When the ATF senior leadership went before a Congressional committee to explain its investigation of the Branch Davidian group in Waco that ultimately led to 86 deaths, including 4 ATF agents in 1993, the Congressional report concluded, among other things that:[16]

> The affidavit filed in support of the ATF's arrest and search warrants included knowingly false statements;

The BATF fraudulently claimed that the Branch Davidians were producing methamphetamine, in order to obtain non-reimbursable and prompt military support;

The BATF's military-style raid was deeply flawed, in concept, in planning, and in execution;

The decision to end the standoff on April 19, 1993, was ``premature, wrong, and highly irresponsible.''

The report issued after the collapse of Fast & Furious basically said the same thing, but once congressional Republicans realized they could not directly link Obama to the death of Border Agent Brian Terry, they lost interest in pursuing further action against ATF, basically allowing the agency to initiate rather benign internal discipline against mid-level managers in the Tucson field office and Washington, D.C. I am not a believer in coincidences as proving anything other than a coincidence, but I can't help but assume the existence of some connection between how the ATF dealt with Dave Laguercia before and after Sandy Hook, and the fact that a lawsuit had just been filed charging the agency with negligence in the death of Brian Terry, which once again created media interest in the inability of the ATF to properly manage an investigation into the illegal use of guns.

But perhaps the answer as to why Dave went from being just another gun dealer who couldn't keep his records straight to the dealer whose behavior reflected a propensity and risk to commit serious crimes, was not so much due to the specific act of selling the AR-15 to Nancy Lanza, but to the fact that he would not have been able to sell her the gun if the ATF had been unwilling to countenance his continued and willful violation of regulatory rules and had shut him down in 2008 or 2010 for the same violations which got him revoked in 2012.

Imagine what would have happened if Dave had become an obsessive, record-keeping fiend after his first inspection, created a foolproof process for insuring that every form was filled out perfectly, every dot in the right place, every crossing of every t. Imagine if the dealer who had then sold the AR-15 to Nancy Lanza couldn't have been pictured as a 'rogue' dealer with what one media source claimed was a 'troubled history,' a headline based entirely on misleading information leaked to the media by the ATF?

If this had been the case after December 14, 2012 the ATF and the government wouldn't have been able to show any kind of response at all to the horrific murders of 20 children and 6 adults in the elementary school at Sandy Hook. Which is why some kind of conspiracy was launched on or before December 20 that wrecked the business and personal life of the dealer who transferred the killing weapon to the mother of the killer in a completely legal sale. But as we shall see in the chapter which follows, this conspiracy was small potatoes compared to the conspiracy theories which were then to come.

CHAPTER 6

WHAT HAPPENED AT SANDY HOOK

In the obituary for attorney Mark Lane, who died in May 2016 at the age of 89, the New York Times estimated that more than 2,000 books had been published for and against the idea of a conspiracy surrounding the assassination of President John F. Kennedy in 1963.[1] The reason for this comment appearing in Lane's death notice was that he was the most prolific and active Kennedy conspiracy theorist of all time.

We do not have a Mark Lane for what happened at Sandy Hook, if only because as horrific an event as it was, you cannot compare the public response to what happened in Newtown on December 14, 2016, to what did or didn't take place in Dallas on November 22, 1963. Nevertheless, the Sandy Hook massacre has spawned a small, cottage industry of conspiracy theories and theorists, and if we going to consider how the ATF may have created a false narrative about Dave Laguercia and his alleged responsibility for what happened in Newtown, we also need to consider how and why other false Newtown narratives emerged.

To begin, even before David Laguercia was initially tied to Sandy Hook through a mid-afternoon trace inquiry from the ATF, media reports were beginning to appear about the Sandy Hook massacre which were, if not erroneous, then certainly incomplete. The best summary of the torrent of inaccurate reporting which flooded the media within moments after the shooting and then continued for days afterwards was a website headline on NPR: "Nearly everyone reported so many things wrong in the first 24 hours after the Sandy Hook shootings that it's hard to single out any one news organization or reporter for criticism."[2] The piece went on to mention such professional organizations as CBS, Associated Press, The New York Times and NPR for getting their reportage more wrong than right.

The first mistake was a 3 P.M. story on Fox News which identified the shooter as Ryan Lanza, who in fact was Adam's older brother, working in New York City and living across the Hudson River in New Jersey. The wrong identity was given to Fox by a cop because, for reasons we will never know, Adam Lanza happened to be carrying his brother's driver's license with him when he drove from his house to the school. A second, equally erroneous story cited by NPR was that the school principal, Dawn Hochsburg, heard someone knocking at the front door, went to the entrance, recognized Adam from a visit he made to the school the previous day and let him enter the building. This story was also totally untrue, but once media outlets began issuing corrections to both statements, the damage was done.

The point is that what created the confusion which then allowed endless suspicions that morphed into totally-false conspiracy theories was not inaccurate reporting per se, but the fact that the various media outlets then stumbled over each other correcting their mistakes, changing their stories, revising their stories, thus giving the clear impression that they could not be trusted to come up with a complete or factual explanation of the events at Sandy Hook.

But throwing out misleading or incomplete news reports was one thing, consciously creating a wholly fabricated theory which attempted to deny the shooting itself was something else. And as far as I am able to track down the genesis of these latter accounts, an early summary of initial Sandy Hook deniers appears to have been put online December 20, 2012 by James Tracy, a Professor of

Communications at Florida Atlantic University, who cobbled together a bunch of Youtube videos which started appearing almost immediately after the massacre and promoted the idea that the massacre had actually been the work of multiple shooters whose existence, let alone identity, was being kept under wraps.[3]

An alternate theory which entirely discounted any shooting incident at Sandy Hook began to emerge on the InfoWars website, which posted several of the amateur videos already getting traction on various Youtube sites.[4] The InfoWars video also featured a rambling monologue by Alex Jones which connected the alleged 'suppression' of what really happened at Sandy Hook back to the attempt by Warner Bros. to keep Jones from posting a review of the Batman movie, *The Dark Night Rises*, that was showing in the Aurora Century 16 when James Holmes walked in during the midnight show and killed or wounded more than 80 theatergoers. What did this all demonstrate to Alex Jones? That neither the shooting at Aurora or the shooting at Sandy Hook ever took place.

The publication of articles, blogs videos and books denying the Sandy Hook massacre will never match the proliferation of JFK-assassination conspiracy publications, but a comprehensive summary and collection of publications from the Sandy Hook denier community can be found in a downloadable book, *Nobody Died At Sandy Hook*, edited by Jim Fetzer and Jim Palecek. The latter author is a long-time pacifist and anti-war activist, the former a retired Professor of Philosophy at the University of Minnesota who has also published a book denying that the 1993 bombing at the Boston Marathon actually took place.[5]

The sub-title of this Sandy Hook denier compendium, however, *It Was a FEMA Drill to Promote Gun Control,* gets to the core issue motivating Sandy Hook deniers, namely, the belief that mass shootings during the Obama Administration were used as part of an overarching conspiracy to eradicate the protections of the 2nd Amendment and rid the country of guns. The alleged existence of a second shooter at Newtown, which was the centerpiece of the initial denier video reports, perfectly fits a common theme found in other high-profile shooting events, according to James Tracy: "It is now beyond question that the assassinations of John F. Kennedy, Robert F. Kennedy, and Martin Luther King Jr. all involved patsies, additional gunman and perhaps most importantly, mass media complicity to achieve their political ends."

But the connection between these shootings and what happened at Sandy Hook cannot be made through the occurrence or non-occurrence of the shootings themselves because it is simply not possible to argue that the Kennedy Brothers and Dr. King survived the assassination attempts the way it is being argued that nobody died at Sandy Hook. Rather, the existence of more than one shooter who then conveniently disappears is 'proof' that an event is being 'stage-managed,' regardless of whether actual shootings occur or not. In the case of Newtown, once you admit that the event was planned, then you can basically come up with any scenario you want. And it is not by accident that the scenario which drives Sandy Hook conspiracy theories is based on the gun control narrative, because the pro-gun community has been promoting its own conspiratorial views of gun control for decades prior to the mass shooting at Newtown on December 14, 2012.

If you don't recognize the phrase, 'slippery slope,' then you haven't received a fund-raising pitch from the NRA. At least since the early 1980's, which is when I started reading my NRA mail, the gun-rights organization never lets an opportunity slide by without reminding its members and gun owners in general that any gun-control measures at the federal or state levels, no matter how seemingly benign or well-intended, is a 'slippery slope' that will sooner or later lead to 2nd-Amendment restrictions and ultimately outright confiscation of guns.

What happens after the government seizes the guns? Martial law is imposed, Constitutional freedoms are abolished, democracy withers away and is replaced by tyranny or worse. What was the first thing the Nazis did after coming to power? They banned guns. Actually, what the Nazis really did was to selectively enforce a gun registration law against certain 'subversive' elements (Communists, Jews) that had been passed under the Weimar government, but why quibble over a few misplaced facts?[6] Indeed, there wouldn't have been a Holocaust had the Jews been armed and therefore been better able to resist the *Wehrmacht*; after all, anyone with a Mauser rifle was certainly able to take out a tank.

What's interesting about the slippery-slope conspiracy theory, of course, is it only seems to operate when Democrats are in control. When a Republican occupies the Oval Office, there doesn't seem to be any concern about government tyranny or the erosion of Constitutional rights. And it just so happens that when a Republican happens to be in the White House, and particularly if a Republican is living at 1600 Pennsylvania Avenue while one or both

Congressional chambers are also controlled by the GOP, that none of the stalwart defenders of the 2nd Amendment seem overly worried about either losing their guns or the possibility that once their guns disappear, that their freedom will disappear as well.

In fact, the only two occasions when the federal government passed any gun-control laws following World War II (1968, 1994) was when the Democrats were the majority in both the Senate and the House, and the President was a liberal who happened to be from the South. Neither of those two political circumstances existed in the aftermath of Sandy Hook. The Democrats held a 55-45 margin in the Senate, although 60 votes were needed to advance legislation to the floor for a vote; the GOP held a slight 30-seat majority in the House. On the other hand, the President was about as far away from being a Southerner, liberal or otherwise, as any President could be. Which meant that any attempt to get gun-control legislation to his desk would probably fail, which it did.

Conspiracy theorists had been building a following since well before Sandy Hook, but the events in Newtown around December 14, 2012 were tailor-made for this audience given the degree to which many of them were already committed to a conspiratorial perspective when it came to the issue of guns. And what made this particular conspiracy somewhat plausible, was not only the fact that demands for stricter gun control were immediately raised within the government and without, but the three most visible individuals leading the charge for stricter laws each had an unquestioned pedigree as an 'enemy' of guns.

Obama, of course, got himself into hot water during the 2008 primary campaign when he shot his mouth off at a fundraiser about how all those people living in small towns where you would never find arugula on a restaurant menu (never mind a restaurant) couldn't stop 'clinging' to their religion or their guns. In his years in the Senate, Biden had been a sponsor or co-sponsor of every gun bill, including the infamous assault weapons ban in 1994. As for Eric Holder, in 1995 while he was U.S. Attorney for the District of Columbia, he delivered a speech in which he suggested that schoolchildren be given a daily lesson in the risks from guns which, as you can imagine, went over like a lead balloon with the pro-gun crowd but resurfaced again once conspiracy theories began swirling around Sandy Hook.[7]

Nobody would ever try to argue that these conspiracy theories, then or now, contain even a grain of truth. The fact that so many of these theories attached themselves to Sandy Hook, however, is not a function of whether they contain a rational or reasonable argument to explain what really happened in Newtown on December 14, rather their continued survival reflects the degree to which public authorities – government, law enforcement, health – have been unable to present a conclusive or even believable analysis as to why this event and other rampage shootings actually take place.

The official report about Sandy Hook released by the State of Connecticut almost a year after the rampage, contained endless and comprehensive details about the timeline of the shootings, the names and descriptions of victims, the responses by various first-responder teams and a specific analysis of how and why it was determined that Adam Lanza acted entirely on his own. To have 'stage-managed' an event of this magnitude, someone or some agency or some inter-galactic presence would have been required to make sure that representatives from at least 18 different federal, state and local agencies and administrative bodies would have told the same bunch of made-up nonsense to the group which compiled this report, a group, incidentally, which was headed by the Connecticut State's Attorney's office in Danbury.

But despite the reams of evidence, photographs and video/audio files which were included in the report, when we get to the explanation as to why Adam Lanza walked into the school on December 14 and began blasting away, the certainty and the undeniable conclusiveness of this mass of evidence disappears. What we are left with is nothing more than vague assumptions and assertions about why the shooter did what he did. Here's the operative statement:

> What we do know is that the shooter had significant mental health issue that, while not affecting the criminality of the shooter's mental state for his crimes or his criminal responsibility for them, did affect his ability to live a normal life and to interact with others, even those to whom he should have been close. *Whether this contributed in any way is unknown.* [my italics.]

Let's return for a minute to the videos posted by Elliott Rodger on the days leading up to his rampage at Isla Vista which we mentioned back in Chapter 1. In the aftermath of this event, mental health experts pointed out that these videos might have been a harbinger of the murders Rodger then committed because these statements contained graphic, personal statements indicating both Rodger's anguish and anger at his inability to engage peers, particularly female peers, in normal, everyday life. Eric Harris filled a website with similar complaints and threats in the period leading up the Columbine attack. James Holmes mentioned his desire to 'kill people' while he was dating a young woman who then decided that he didn't represent the kind of company that she wanted to keep. In none of these personal histories can a specific lever or event be identified which pushed any of these obviously unstable individuals to cross the line from thought to action and commit mass murder at the time they did.

In the report on Adam Lanza's mental status that was submitted by the Connecticut Office of Child Advocate, an example of the kind of behavior that should have alerted people to the shooter's oncoming decision to commit his spectacularly violent event was the fact that he was engrossed in reading the 1,500-page *European Declaration of Independence* which was written and then published online by Anders Breivik, a self-employed techie who holds the world record for the number of mass shooting victims which he set at a summer camp outside of Oslo on July 22, 2011.[8]

I don't know anyone other than myself and Adam Lanza who might have read this entire document, but while it was the handiwork of a mass shooter, we might actually say *the* mass shooter, there is no mention within the entire text about plans or ideas to commit individual mass murder or any act of physical violence at all. While the text goes into great detail about planning and executing physical attacks on what Breivik refers to as the European elites which promote 'multiculturalism' in order to oppress the average man, these attacks are all going to be carried out by organized, militia-style groups whose purpose is to defend Western (i.e., white, Christian) culture against the Marxists and their Muslim allies in a future civil war.

Does the content of Breivik's manifesto differ substantially from what could be considered as the description of a culturally-incorrect video game? Not really, and Lanza was hardly the first mass shooter to spend hours in front of an X-box or a computer monitor playing digital war and shooting games. If the authorities had wanted to 'stage-manage' a mass shooting in Newtown in order to carry out this contrived event, they would have had no difficulty identifying any number of late-adolescent boys who spent their time at home or at a video arcade pretending that what they were playing was a dress rehearsal for the real thing.

All of which brings us back to the fact that within several days after December 14, the government, and in particular the ATF, realized they were sitting on a powder-keg because of what they learned once they reviewed the transactions that allowed Nancy Lanza to purchase two guns which her son then had with him when he burst into the school. Recall that it was Laguercia who informed the ATF on December 14 that Nancy Lanza hadn't purchased one gun from Riverview Sales, in fact she had purchased two. And more to the point, one of those guns, which the ATF had not yet linked to Riverview when they called with their trace request was the AR-15, the weapon that was used to kill 6 adults and 20 school kids. In fact, the gun which had first put Riverview on the ATF's radar screen was the Sig 226 pistol which Lanza took with him to the school but never used.

When the ATF began reviewing the 4473 forms which they had taken out of Dave's store, they discovered that the employee who had actually sold the AR-15 to Nancy Lanza was the same employee, Krys Dibella, whom Laguerca had later fired after the ATF informed him that Dibella had possibly committed a felony by selling ammunition to someone he knew to be prohibited from purchasing or possessing either guns or ammunition because he admitted to having been convicted of a felony at an earlier point in time. And this discovery created not one, but two problems for the ATF.

First, when Dibella entered the background check information into the 4473, he dated the call to FBI-NICS differently from the date at which the gun was actually out into Nancy Lanza's hands. This discrepancy had been noticed by the lead ATF inspector, Tim Gahn, who flagged this violation when the report on that inspection was being prepared. The violation was then noted in the documentation that was used to justify the FFL revocation action which led to the August 8-9 Boston meeting.

But much more worrisome for the ATF was the fact that not only had Krys Dibella possibly committed a felony by selling ammunition to a 'prohibited person,' but this sale occurred during the time-period when the ATF knew about Dibella's illegal ammunition sale but had not informed Laguercia that such an event had taken place. In other words, when Nancy Lanza purchased the AR, the guy who sold her the gun shouldn't have been selling guns or working in Riverview at all. And this information, which would have tied the ATF to Sandy Hook rather than Laguercia, was staring the ATF in the face when they examined the relevant 4473 which Dave had willingly handed over that Sunday afternoon.

The time-line of these events cannot be disputed, and if there was any 'stage-managing' at Sandy Hook, this management had nothing to do with inventing a mass shooting but it had *everything* to do with inventing someone who could be viewed by the public as somehow responsible for what happened on December 14. And the ATF stage management began on the afternoon of December 20 when the upcoming raid on Riverview Sales was leaked to the media who were standing around the Newtown Fire Department while Holder, Malloy and ATF officials were meeting inside.

Like all attempts to turn truth into fiction, in this case a perfectly-legal sale of a perfectly-legal gun, sooner or later the problems created by the conspiracy begin to come out.

By telling media representatives like Len Besthoff about a police action in which a warrant was going to be served, the ATF violated the most basic communications protocol that is always followed prior to an action of this kind. Every law enforcement agency and officer knows that if an intended target of a raid finds out that the cavalry is going to show up, the first thing which happens is the destruction of the evidence for which the warrant has been drawn to justify the search. In this case, of course, the ATF didn't have to worry about whether Laguercia would destroy any incriminating evidence, because on two, separate occasions he had already voluntarily produced all the evidence which tied him to Sandy

Hook. And if someone at the ATF Hartford office was dumb enough to believe that maybe by diligently searching the records they might find more illegal transfers of guns, given the presentation of the results of the latest inspection during the Boston meeting of August 8-9, what more evidence could they possibly need?

Maybe the reason why more than 20 agents, some carrying weapons and all dressed in tactical gear charged into Riverview was the mistaken belief that if they pulled the store completely apart perhaps they would discover a hidden cache of illegal guns. If that were the case, how was it that at no time in the previous ten years had Riverview been considered a source of crime guns? In fact, the only real crimes involving guns at Riverview were when guns were stolen from the shop without either Dave or other employees realizing that such events had occurred.

But let's go back to the stage-management of the raid and look at it from a different point of view. Is it beyond the realm of possibility that when Besthoff tweeted about the upcoming raid on Riverview that the text might have been picked up by the alt-right social media and blasted around to various, pro-gun outlets, then resulting in the appearance of a group of armed vigilantes or patriots, depending on which definition you prefer, who would have tried to defend

Laguercia against the loss of his 2nd-Amendment rights?

If you think this is a far-fetched notion concocted simply to besmirch the reputations of the dedicated officials of the ATF, I urge you to recall what happened when the law showed up with a warrant for Arizona rancher Clive 'let me tell you about your Negro' Bundy, or what happened when his sons took temporary possession of the Malheur National Forest admin building in Oregon and, once again, the alt-right, gun-loving social media universe exploded with calls for America's most dedicated defenders to show up with their guns and protect the Constitution from being trampled by a group of law enforcement officers representing the feds.[10]

If the ATF or local police officials had any reason to suspect that Laguercia or anyone else working at Riverview might have been a threat to the safety of the individuals who stormed in waving their warrant in the air, it is simply beyond my imagination that they would have been so stupid and careless as to make a public announcement about the raid before it occurred. What really happened, I suspect, is that the purpose of the raid was to show the public that the government was making some kind of response to what had occurred the previous week at Sandy Hook, which at least would create the impression that the mass shootings did not represent the kind of unchecked and unprotected violent events which many Americans now believed them to be.

Imagine on the other hand, if there had been no campaign to discredit Laguercia and link him to Sandy Hook. Imagine on the other hand if the public had learned that the killing gun had been sold to Nancy Lanza by an individual whose felonious behavior had not only been known by the ATF but had been kept from being disclosed to his employer for nearly one year. Coming on the heels of the lawsuit filed by Brian Terry's family alleging misconduct by senior field management of the ATF, imagine the reaction had it become known that the same law enforcement agency had failed to take any measures to prevent an individual suspected of committing a felony crime involving guns to the point that he was allowed to sell more than 3,000 additional guns after he sold the AR-15 that was used at Sandy Hook.

What we have here is not some fanciful, conspiracy theory being peddled by hucksters like Alex Jones who make a living by exploiting the fears and paranoia of people who truly believe that the Martians have landed at Area 51. It's easy for rational-minded people like myself to brush aside the nonsensical claims of people who want to sell the idea that the 28 funerals which took place after Sandy

Hook (26 shooting victims plus mother and son Lanza) were all staged so that the Obama administration could go forward with its master plan to confiscate America's guns. But there was, in fact, a conspiracy surrounding Sandy Hook, except it was a conspiracy that rested not on the idea of a stage-managed event which didn't really take place, but a conspiracy which rested on the fact that a terrible event indeed did occur for which the government could not explain the reason for its occurrence and thus provide the public with some kind of reasonable, workable plan for preventing it from happening again. But if the government couldn't come up with a 'why,' given the demise of the actual shooter, at last the government could come up with, and blame a 'who.'

The 'who' in this case, of course, was Dave Laguercia, and from the moment the ATF burst into his gun shop, he became the target of a conscious and ongoing conspiracy to make the public believe that someone was going to suffer in some way for what happened at the Sandy Hook elementary school on December 14. Obviously, the people who suffered worst, indeed indescribably worst, were the adults and children whose lives ended that day. Their families, friends and community continue to bear suffering to a degree that cannot be imagined by anyone else. But Nancy and Adam Lanza were also victims – she at the hands of her son, he driven to take his own life by the same emotional demons which pushed him to snuff out so many other lives.

Which left Dave – the guy who sold the gun. The guy whose lack of paperwork skills posed a threat to community safety which is why the ATF shut him down. Why did the ATF overlook these same errors for four years and allow Dave Laguercia to continue to run his gun shop and sell 5,000 or more guns every year? Because until they realized how vulnerable they were after Dave produced the 4473 paperwork covering Nancy Lanza's purchase of an AR-15, it never occurred to them that Dave represented any kind of threat to community safety at all. In fact, he did not.

POSTSCRIPT

I wrote this book for two reasons:

(1). I wanted to make readers aware of the degree to which mass shootings, and gun violence in general, are not behaviors which are capable of any realistic solution as long as the individuals who commit this violence have little or no difficulty getting their hands on guns. And the idea that all we have to do is figure out and implement policies that will restrict the ownership of guns to what we call the 'law-abiding' population is an idea completely detached from reality because, for example, Nancy Lanza and for that matter her son Adam were as law-abiding as two people could be.

The only people who have come up with a diagnosis of mass shooters which reinforces the stereotype that they are all loonies in disguise, are the writers for pop magazines like *Psychology Today* and other popular publications who are paid to come up with some kind of reason why these events occur, notwithstanding the fact that when competent mental health professionals evaluate the occasional person who survives his own shooting rampage, invariably they are judged to be rational and sane. Once their basic sanity has been established, then the experts fall back on the idea that some event occurred which briefly, impulsively, pushed them over the edge. The fact is that the exact same argument can be made to explain why someone shoots themselves or someone else with a gun in America more than 300 times every day.

(2). I also wrote this book because Dave Laguercia not only needed someone to speak out on his behalf, but we also need to step back and take a long, hard look at the manner in which the agency that is responsible for regulating firearms in this country does and doesn't do its job. The ATF investigators who came into Riverview Sales and go into every licensed gun shop to conduct an examination of the relevant paperwork (A&D book and 4473 forms) are not law enforcement personnel, they don't wear shields or carry guns. They are basically glorified, self-important clerks, no different in terms of the tasks they actually perform than what someone does who comes into a law firm and copy-edits the day's depositions to make sure there are no grammatical or spelling mistakes.

But there is, in fact, a very important difference between an ATF audit and, for example, the accountant who came into Riverview, sat down and verified the store's daily, monthly or yearly receipts. And the difference is that if the accountant adds up a string of numbers and something's out of whack, all he needs to do is go back, find the number which was written down incorrectly, change it to the correct number and add up the column again. But if an ATF inspector walks into Riverview or any licensed gun dealer and discovers that a 4473 form was dated incorrectly or that the caliber of a particular gun was entered in the wrong space, what he is looking at is not a piece of information that can easily be erased and changed; he's looking at something which, under statute, constitutes a criminal offense.

When Dave Laguercia stood up in Federal Court on March 27, 2014 and was sentenced to three years' probation, community service and a fine for making two mistakes on two separate forms, he could have been indicted and sentenced for every single one of the thousands of clerical errors which the ATF found in the three inspections that were carried out at Riverview Sales. And yet the truth is that Dave would never have been in court, would never have suffered the entire loss of his business, never mind the character assassinations he endured because of the leaks to the press, had the ATF conducted a trace of the Sig 226 pistol on December 14 and ended up talking to some dealer in some other shop.

When the word got around to other gun dealers like myself that the AR used at Sandy Hook had come out of Riverview Sales, I can guarantee you that every, single gun dealer, myself included, felt bad for Dave and at the same time thought, 'better him than me.' No gun dealer who sold that AR-15 to Nancy Lanza, no matter how legal the sale, was going to escape unscathed, a sad but true commentary on how the government goes about regulating guns.

Mass shootings are Black Swans: totally unpredictable, random, catastrophic events.[1] Anyone who believes that it might be possible develop a profile which could then be used in some way to identify individuals at risk for such inexplicable behavior is looking for a needle in a haystack, except the haystack doesn't exist. How do we know whether young men suffering from serious, perhaps incapacitating mental distress who end up in treatment and then go on to lead normal, productive lives, would otherwise have committed a shooting rampage because they didn't get help? We keep attempting to mitigate somehow the dangers represented by such individuals even though it is simply impossible to know or predict the next Black Swan rampage event. It won't work.

One more point about these mass shootings before we once again turn the spotlight on Dave. In fact, there is no agreement in law enforcement, public health or psychiatry regarding the definition of an event like Sandy Hook. Some call it a 'mass' shooting, others call it a 'rampage,' and some use both terms interchangeably because we don't really know how to create an analytical shoe, so to speak, that can fit on every foot. The shooting incidents that I discussed in this book, however, share certain characteristics which are different from most other mass shootings which seem to occur to a degree in this country which is simply unthinkable anywhere else.

First, most mass shooting experts define these events as resulting in 4 deaths or more. This book only discusses 6 mass shootings which resulted in 106 persons killed, an average of almost 18 deaths per shooting. In his well-researched book *Rampage Nation*, Louis Klarevas sets his minimum mass shooting at 6 per event, and between 1966 (Whitman) and the end of 2015, he believes there has been 111 such shootings, for an average of 8 deaths per event. Had Klaveras defined mass shootings as 4 or more deaths, which is the number usually proposed both by lay experts and the cops, he would have ended up with at least double the number that he claims – this book looks only at the exceptional, spectacular events.

In addition to the numeric toll of what happened at places like Columbine, Aurora and Sandy Hook, there is another important factor which sets these events apart from other times when multiple people are gunned down. Most mass shootings are no different from the one-on-one shooting which happens more than 200 times every day insofar as the shooter and his victims had a prior relationship which had been ongoing well before the event. Whether the shooter walks into a family gathering and starts banging away, or like Omar Thornton in Connecticut or Gian Ferri in San Francisco there was a business or employer-employee relationship, the perpetrator in most mass shootings aims his gun at someone he knows.

This is not the usual profile in instances where a lot of people get mowed down. Of the cases described in this book, only Harris and Klebold knew some of their victims and the two students who recognized and conversed with them both then escaped harm. Seung-Hui Cho went into random classrooms on the Virginia Tech campus; Elliott Rodger had absolutely no idea who he was firing at while driving around town; for sure Charley Whitman couldn't have begun to identify any of his targets;

James Holmes couldn't have cared less about who was sitting in the seats at the Century 16; and Adam Lanza went into rooms where he heard voices, not because he recognized anyone at all.

This is what makes these particular events so scary and create such concern in the public mind. Because the circumstances which surround most mass shootings can usually be explained by the fact that the shooter held some kind of grudge or anger at the person or persons whom he ended up taking out. Which doesn't mean we understand how the grudge or the anger spills over into a frenzy of violence, but here again we have to be careful with how we choose our words. Was Charles Whitman sitting up in the Texas Tower feeling particularly angry, or was he carefully and methodically concentrating on hitting the targets no matter how far away? Did Adam Lanza shoot his way into Sandy Hook Elementary School all the while thinking about how much he hated the people inside, or was he carefully acting out a script which he had been creating to use on this particular day?

We don't know the answers to these questions, which is why events like Sandy Hook fill us with fear and dread. And because we are filled with fear, well-meaning individuals in places of public responsibility feel it is necessary to help us believe that something can and will be done. So with all best intentions they create a looking-glass story and if the story happens to land on the head of someone who in some way or another isn't helping to advance the common good, if nothing else maybe they got rid of a pest who otherwise would just be making trouble and standing in the way.

From the moment the ATF burst into Riverview on December 20, 2012, Dave Laguercia felt himself to be in the midst of an Alice-in-Wonderland pageant that only ended when his three-year probation drew to a close. And the moment in all of this when he truly felt he was watching events through the looking-glass was not when he was served a search warrant for

paperwork that he had already freely delivered, not when he read in the newspapers that he was suspected of committing multiple crimes, not even when his wife sat across the table from a federal prosecutor who told her that she could also be facing charges if she didn't start revealing all the illegal activities that she had seen Dave committing in the shop.

The real looking-glass moment came when Dave was given permission by his probation officer to make a thirty-mile journey from his residence in Massachusetts down to Hartford, CT, to attend a required class in transitioning from being incarcerated to living in the outside world, despite the fact that he hadn't spent a single minute of his entire life in jail. Nevertheless, as a probationer he still had to attend the class and he also was required to get permission from his probation officer in order to leave the state in which he lived – Massachusetts – and go to the class in another state – Connecticut – and then had to check in with the probation officer again to tell her that he had returned home.

Dave drove down to Hartford that day, walked into the classroom, found a seat in the corner and from the bits of conversation he picked up from the guys around him, it appeared to be the case that he was the only person in the room who hadn't just left jail after serving hard time for one or multiple serious crimes. And in addition to telling each other why they had done time and how much time they had done, his classmates alternately talked about where weapons were stashed in the various prisons or where after class they were going to score drugs.

Then the door opened, a grotesquely overweight Black man lumbered in, read names from a roster (roughly half the names he called out belonged to guys who hadn't shown up) and then proceeded to lecture the group on what they needed to do in order to look for a job. This was the moment when Dave truly believed that what happened to him beginning on December 14, 2012, could never be rationally understood or explained. Nor for that matter would he ever understand what had happened at Sandy Hook. With those thoughts in his head, the class ended, the former gun dealer Dave Laguercia stood up, walked out of the room and went home.

NOTES

CHAPTER 1

1. Connecticut Department of Emergency Service and Protection, *Sandy Hook Elementary School Shooting Reports.* Online: http://cspsandyhookreport.ct.gov/, accessed July 27, 2016.

2. Andrew Solomon, "The Reckoning, The father of the Sandy Hook killer searches for answers, The New Yorker Magazine, March 17, 2014. Online:

http://www.newyorker.com/magazine/2014/03/17/the-reckoning, accessed July16, 2017.

3. Adam Lanza's developmental history which is covered in pages 9 through 11, is drawn primarily from, State of Connecticut Office of Child Advocate, Shooting At Sandy Hook Elementary School, November 21, 2014, Online: http://www.ct.gov/oca/lib/oca/sandyhook11212014.pdf, accessed June 24, 2017. This information is also found in the official state report on Sandy Hook: State of Connecticut, Division of Criminal Justice, Report of the State's Attorney for the Judicial District of Danbury on the Shootings at Sandy Hook Elementary School and 36 Yogananda Street, Newtown, Connecticut on December 14, 2012,

http://www.ct.gov/csao/lib/csao/Sandy_Hook_Final_Report.pdf, accessed June 16, 2017.

4. The discussion of Virginia Tech, pages 11 – 15, is found in, Report of the Virginia Tech Review Panel Presented to Timothy M. Kaine, Governor, Commonwealth of Virginia, August, 2007. https://governor.virginia.gov/media/3772/fullreport.pdf, accessed July 3, 2017. Additional material found in the *Addendum to the Review Panel Report,*

http://scholar.lib.vt.edu/prevail/docs/April16ReportRev200912
04.pdf, accessed June 16,2007.

5.   *The New York Times*, April 18, 2007,
https://thelede.blogs.nytimes.com/2007/04/18/virginia-
massacre-day-three/, accessed July11, 2017.

6.   Information about Aurora shooting from numerous media
reports (several cited below) plus, System Planning Corporation,
*Aurora Century 16 Theater Shooting, After Action Report for the City of
Aurora, CO.*

https://www.courts.state.co.us/Media/Opinion_Docs/14CV31
595%20After%20Action%20Review%20Report%20Redacted.pd
f, accessed July 2, 2017.

7.   Dale Archer, "James Holmes: A Psychiatric Analyis,"
Psychology Today, January 27, 2015,
https://www.psychologytoday.com/blog/reading-between-the-
headlines/201501/james-holmes-psychiatric-analysis,   accessed
June 23, 2017. Also see Jamie Turndorf, "Was Adam Lanza an
Undiagnosed Schizophrenic," Psychology Today, December 20,
2012, https://www.psychologytoday.com/blog/we-can-work-it-
out/201212/was-adam-lanza-undiagnosed-schizophrenic,
accessed June 21, 2017.

8.   A conference held at Yale University on April 20, 2017 on
the mental state of President Trump was criticized by many
professionals in the mental health community for violating the
Goldwater 'rule' since none of the conference participants had,
in fact, met with or diagnosed Trump,

http://www.independent.co.uk/news/world-0/donald-trump-
dangerous-mental-illness-yale-psychiatrist-conference-us-
president-unfit-james-gartner-a7694316.html,   accessed   July7,
2017.

9.   http://www.denverpost.com/2015/06/16/aurora-theater-shooting-gunman-told-doctor-you-cant-kill-everyone/

10.   Description of the Santa Isla shooting (pages 20-22) from, Santa Barbara County Sheriff's Office, *Isla Vista Mass Murder, May 23, 2014, Investigative Summary,*

http://www.sbsheriff.us/documents/ISLAVISTAINVESTIGA TIVESUMMARY.pdf, accessed June 12, 2017.

11.   Berit Brogaard, "Elliot Rodger's Narcissism," *Psychology Today*, June 4, 2014,

https://www.psychologytoday.com/blog/the-mysteries-love/201406/elliot-rodger-s-narcissism, accessed July 6, 2017.

12.   Description of Columbine events (pages 21-25) from, State of Colorado, *The Report of Governor Bill Owens' Columbine Review Commission,* May, 2001,

https://schoolshooters.info/sites/default/files/Columbine%20-%20Governor's%20Commission%20Report.pdf accessed July 7, 2017.

13.   *ibid.,* pp.19 & 22.

14.   The full text of the report issued after the conference can be downloaded here:

http://files.eric.ed.gov/fulltext/ED446352.pdf.

15.   Emma McGinty and Daniel Webster, "Gun Violence and Serious Mental Illness," in, Liza Gold and Robert Simon, eds, Gun Violence and Mental Illness (Arlington, VA: American Psychiatric Association, 2016), p. 3.

16.   *ibid.,* p. 4.

Chapter 2

1. For details on the rules which comprise the National Firearms Act, see: https://www.atf.gov/qa-category/national-firearms-act-nfa., accessed July 31, 2017.

2. A comprehensive summary of GCA68 can be found in the website of The Law Center To Prevent Gun Violence, http://smartgunlaws.org/gun-laws/federal-law/background-resources/key-federal-acts-regulating-firearms/, accessed July 12, 2017.

3. ATF regulations covering the A&D book: https://www.atf.gov/firearms/docs/atf-national-firearms-act-handbook-chapter-12/download, accessed June 19, 2017.

4. The 4473 form can be downloaded here: https://www.atf.gov/file/61446/download, accessed May 3, 2017.

5. Summary of ATF compliance activity: https://www.atf.gov/file/4796/download, detailed reference of statutes defining ATF regulatory authority: https://www.atf.gov/file/11241/download, both accessed July 30, 2017.

6. https://www.atf.gov/resource-center/fact-sheet/fact-sheet-federal-firearms-compliance-inspections-and-revocation-process.

7. Thornton's rampage was the first mass killing in Connecticut and provoked extensive media coverage: http://www.nbcnews.com/id/38535909/ns/us_news-crime_and_courts/t/dead-shooting-conn-beer-distributor/, accessed June 16, 2017.

8. https://www.americanprogress.org/press/release/2015/0 5/19/113360/release-after-2-year-investigation-cap-report-

concludes-that-atfs-mission-and-agents-should-be-moved-into-the-fbi/, accessed July 13, 2017.

9.   The Washington Times is not known for publishing articles about the gun industry which are even remotely balanced or objective, but this particular story rings true: http://www.washingtontimes.com/news/2014/sep/18/onerous-atf-rules-threaten-to-put-gun-dealers-out-/, accessed July 11, 2017.

10.   https://www.atf.gov/resource-center/fact-sheet/fact-sheet-national-tracing-center, accessed May 6, 2017.

11.   https://www.atf.gov/about/firearms-trace-data-2015, accessed May 6, 2017.

Chapter 3

1.   Press Conference, *Report to the Governor, Medical Aspects, Charles J. Whitman Catastrophe, September 8, 1966,*

http://alt.cimedia.com/statesman/specialreports/whitman/findings.pdf.

2.   https://www.thetrace.org/2017/02/remington-settlement-deadly-rifle-defect-too-lenient/ accessed July 16, 2017.

3.   http://www.nytimes.com/1993/07/03/us/the-broker-who-killed-8-gunman-s-motives-a-puzzle.html, accessed June 11, 2017.

4.   A good summary of the assault weapons ban is found here: https://www.washingtonpost.com/news/wonk/wp/2012/12/17/everything-you-need-to-know-about-banning-assault-weapons-in-one-post/?utm_term=.3b4cad2e37ea, accessed June 24, 2017.

5.   Here is the definition of 'firearm' from GCA68: "The term **'firearm'** means (A) any weapon (including a starter gun) which will or is designed to or may readily be converted to expel a

projectile by the action of an explosive; (B) the frame or receiver of any such weapon; (C) any firearm muffler or firearm silencer; or (D) any destructive device. Such term does not include an antique firearm." There is no further mention of how a firearm can be designed in this law, which is quite unlike gun-control statutes in other countries that usually contain details about the types and design of guns that are allowed.

6. http://www.texasmonthly.com/articles/96-minutes/

7. https://www.nssf.org/msr/, accessed July 19, 2017.

8. https://www.fbi.gov/file-repository/active-shooter-study-2000-2013-1.pdf/view, accessed July 6, 2017.

9. There are a number of websites that track gun violence through searching media reports which means that the numbers are usually understated. The tracker for mass shootings is at: https://www.massshootingtracker.org/data, accessed July 20, 2017.

10. A summary of the law and how it has been changed is found here: http://smartgunlaws.org/gun-laws/policy-areas/guns-in-public/guns-in-schools/, accessed June 16, 2017.

11. *op. cit.*, pp. 6 – 9.

Chapter 4

1. A pseudonym is being used.

2. Full text of the President's speech: http://swampland.time.com/2012/12/17/these-tragedies-must-end-obama-promises-change-at-newtown-vigil-but-can-he-deliver/, accessed June 21,2017.

3. Numerous media articles appeared following this shooting, for example:

http://www.nytimes.com/2011/01/09/us/politics/09giffords.html, accessed March 19,2017.

4.   In 1995, Wayne Lapierre referred to the ATF as jack-booted, government thugs' in a fundraising letter to the NRA membership. Former President Bush publicly resigned from the organization following media coverage of the letter, although LaPierre later apologized in a telephone interview: http://www.nytimes.com/1995/05/11/us/letter-of-resignation-sent-by-bush-to-rifle-association.html, accessed June 4, 2017.

5.   In the *Appendix* to the Sandy Hook Official Report (cited above, Chapter 1, note 3) one can find copies of the searh/seizure warrants executed for the Honda Civic which Adam Lanza drove to the school, and the search/seizure warrant executed for the Lanza residence on Yogananda Street. Interestingly, the warrant that was served on Laguercia is not included in this or any other official document stemming from the Sandy Hook shooting, but it did appear on a story from the ABC affiliate, WALB-Channel 10 which, of course, quoted the document out of context to make it appear that the ATF had good cause to revoke Laguercia's license in 2012: http://www.walb.com/story/21937184/documents-detail-why-gun-shop-lost-license, accessed Jule7, 2017.

6.   ATF compliance and revocation regulations found here: https://www.atf.gov/resource-center/fact-sheet/fact-sheet-federal-firearms-compliance-inspections-and-revocation-process, accessed May 21, 2017.

7.   http://www.registercitizen.com/article/RC/20121221/NEWS/312219982, accessed June 14, 2017.

8.   http://nypost.com/2012/12/22/newtown-massacre-rifle-purchased-at-same-gun-shop-as-earlier-kill-spree/, accessed June 14, 2017.

9.   The CAP report was published online complete with a photograph of the front of Riverview Sales even though Laguercia's store was only one of 16 gun shops whose missing or stolen guns were considered examples of this serious threat to public safety: https://www.americanprogress.org/issues/guns-crime/reports/2013/06/18/66693/lost-and-stolen-guns-from-gun-dealers/, accessed April 12, 2017.

10.   The text on pps. 87-90 is drawn from the ATF document given to WALB and referenced above in Fn. 5.

Chapter 5

1.   Note penalties section in Chapter 924:

https://www.gpo.gov/fdsys/pkg/USCODE-2011-title18/pdf/USCODE-2011-title18-partI-chap44-sec924.pdf, accessed July 22, 2017.

2.   https://www.atf.gov/columbus-field-division/pr/federally-licensed-firearms-dealers-sentenced-improper-sales, accessed June 16, 2017.

3.   https://www.nationalschoolshield.org/media/1857/national-school-shield-safeguarding-our-children.pdf, accessed June 4, 2017.

4.   https://www.theguardian.com/world/2013/jan/16/obama-executive-actions-gun-violence, accessed July17, 2017.

5.   https://www.washingtonpost.com/news/post-politics/wp/2013/04/17/manchin-toomey-gun-amendment-fails/?utm_term=.5970c7c041b4, accessed July 14, 2017.

6.   http://www.businessinsider.com/george-zimmermans-website-collected-200000-before-he-shut-it-down-2012-4, accessed July 6, 2017.

7.   https://www.theguardian.com/world/2012/dec/14/brian-terry-family-sue-fast-furious, accessed July 2, 2017.

8.   https://oversight.house.gov/wp-content/uploads/2017/06/FINAL_REPORT_2017.pdf, accessed June 17, 2017, pp. 148 and following.

9. "Fast and Furious: Obstruction of Congress by the Department of Justice," Joint Staff Report – Part III, Committee on Oversight and Reform (June 17, 2017), p. 14.

10. https://www.washingtonpost.com/politics/fast-and-furious-eric-holder-held-in-contempt/2012/06/20/gJQAaEUArV_story.html?utm_term=.8c30e13a6b91, accessed July 16, 2017. In 2014 the contempt citation was dismissed in Federal Court.

11. https://www.washingtonpost.com/politics/fast-and-furious-eric-holder-held-in-contempt/2012/06/20/gJQAaEUArV_story.html?utm_term=.8c30e13a6b91, accessed May 16, 2017. This report also contains a summary of the decision to apply for an OCDTEF wiretap, pp. 147 and what follows.

12. Available on Altchiler's SCRIBD website:
https://www.scribd.com/document/340329649/ROBERT-ALTCHILER-ALTCHILER-LLC, accessed June 16, 2017.

13. As quoted in the article cited above, Chapter 4, note 7.

14. Media reports had Holder's motorcade leaving Newtown after 7 PM but the firehouse meeting ended sometime earlier: http://www.ctpost.com/local/article/Holder-in-Newtown-to-focus-on-gun-violence-4136637.php, accessed Jun 11, 2017.

15. These tweets are all validated, including snapshots, in the pre-sentencing memorandum submitted by Robert Altchiler (see fn. 12 above).

16. Complete text of the report is here:
https://www.congress.gov/congressional-report/106th-congress/house-report/1037/1, accessed June 11, 2017.

Chapter 6

1. Mark Lane obituary:

https://www.nytimes.com/2016/05/13/us/mark-lane-who-asserted-that-kennedy-was-killed-in-conspiracy-dies-at-89.html?_r=0, accessed June 21, 2017.

2. http://www.npr.org/2012/12/18/167466320/coverage-rapid-and-often-wrong-in-tragedys-early-hours, accessed July 20, 2017.

3. http://www.globalresearch.ca/the-newtown-school-tragedy-more-than-one-gunman/5316313, accessed June 16, 2017.

4. https://www.youtube.com/watch?v=8nCFHImNeRw, accessed June 17, 2017.

5. The entire text can be downloaded here:

http://www.rense.com/general96/NobodyDiedAtSandyHook_final.pdf, accessed June 12, 2017.

6. Stephen Halbrook, *Gun Control in the Third Reich: Disarming the Jews and "Enemies of the State,"* (New York, 2013). Halbrook, who is a counsel for the NRA, argues that the Jews might have prevented the slaughter of their entire population had the Nazis not been able to enforce the Weimar gun-control laws against them and members of left-wing parties. Echoing such nonsense might have destroyed the last bit of Presidential credibility that Ben Carson enjoyed prior to the 2016 early primary campaign: https://www.nytimes.com/2015/10/15/opinion/ben-carson-is-wrong-on-guns-and-the-holocaust.html, accessed July 28, 2017.

7. An excerpt of Holder's speech containing the brainwashing comment can be downloaded here:

https://www.youtube.com/watch?v=0nM0asnCXD0, accessed June 21, 2017.

8. https://fas.org/programs/tap/_docs/2083_-_A_European_Declaration_of_Independence.pdf, accessed July 7, 2017.

9. https://www.washingtonpost.com/news/the-fix/wp/2014/04/15/everything-you-need-to-know-about-the-long-fight-between-cliven-bundy-and-the-federal-government/?utm_term=.e90c9b701e9a, accessed July 7, 2016.